40
Unique
Mandalas

Hand-drawn, Nature-inspired

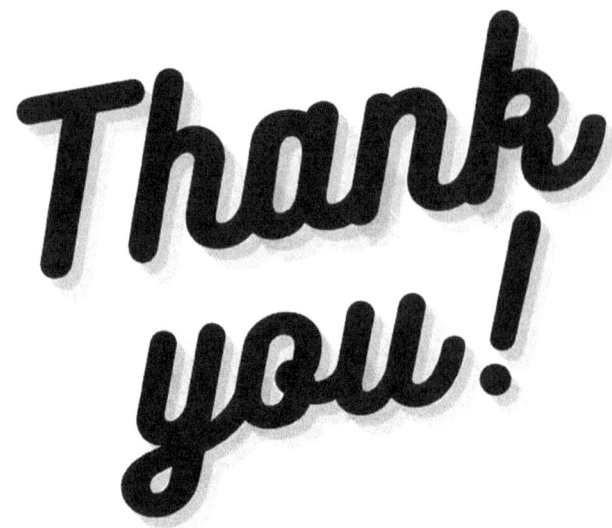

Thank you!

for choosing my coloring book!

I am an artist located in the greater Tacoma area of Washington state in the amazing Pacific Northwest! My work is mainly inspired by the natural world. I hope my art will bring more people to realize how incredibly unique and special our planet is and inspire more folks to help take care of this rarest of homes! I also hope you find a peaceful place inside this book to relax and recharge from your busy lives!

This is my first coloring book of hopefully many to come! I hope you enjoy coloring the intricate patterns and natural themes as much as I enjoyed creating them!

Please leave constructive feedback in the reviews, so I can make my next books better!

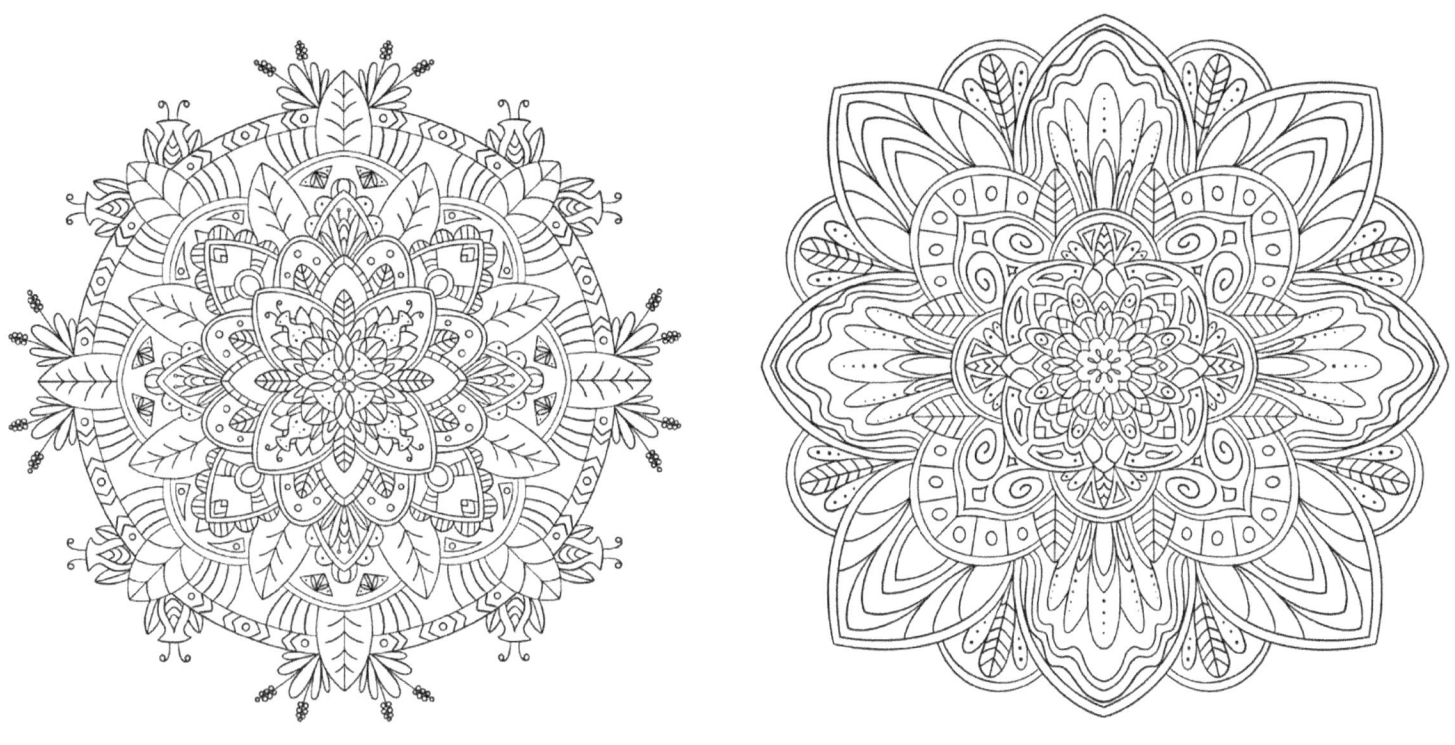

I go to nature to be soothed and healed, and to have my senses put in order.
— John Burroughs

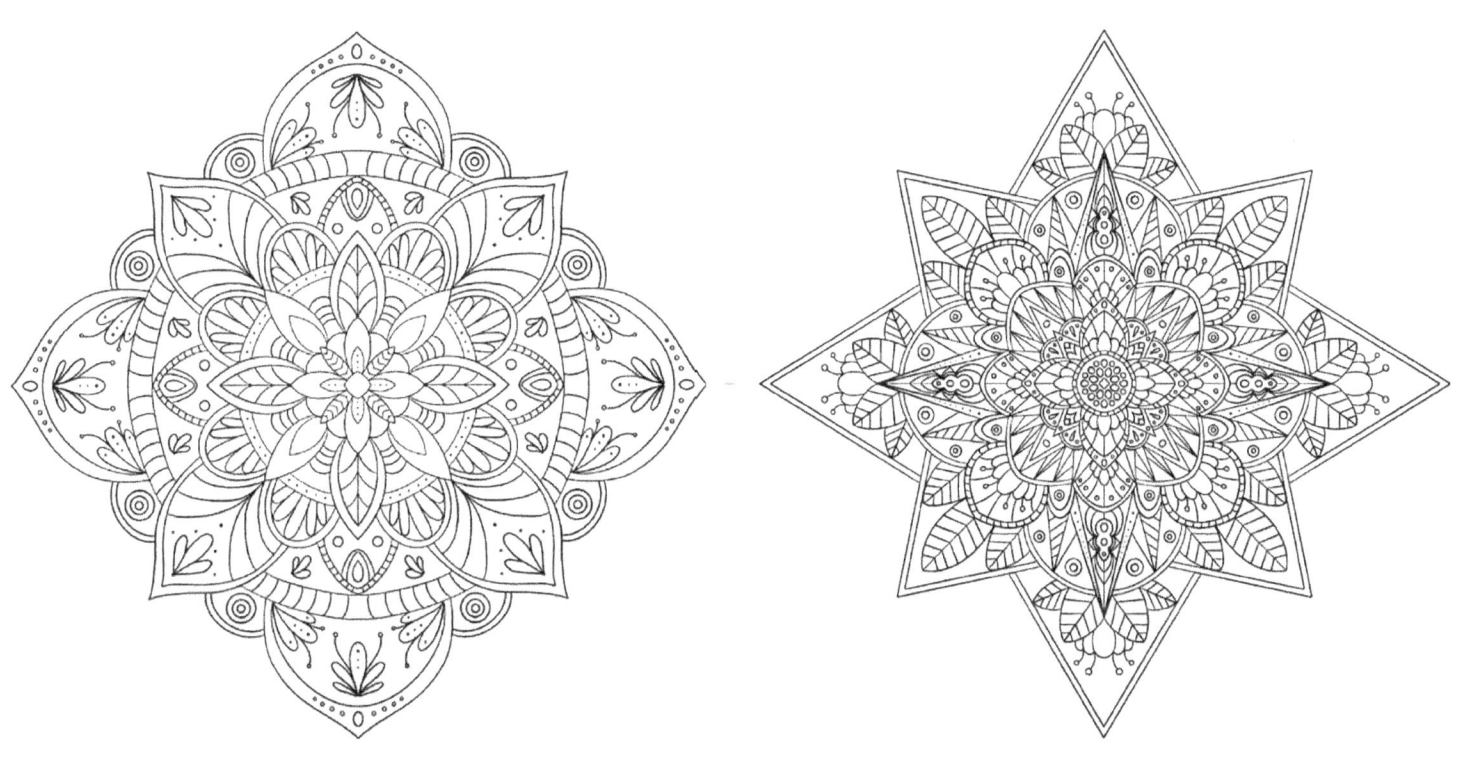

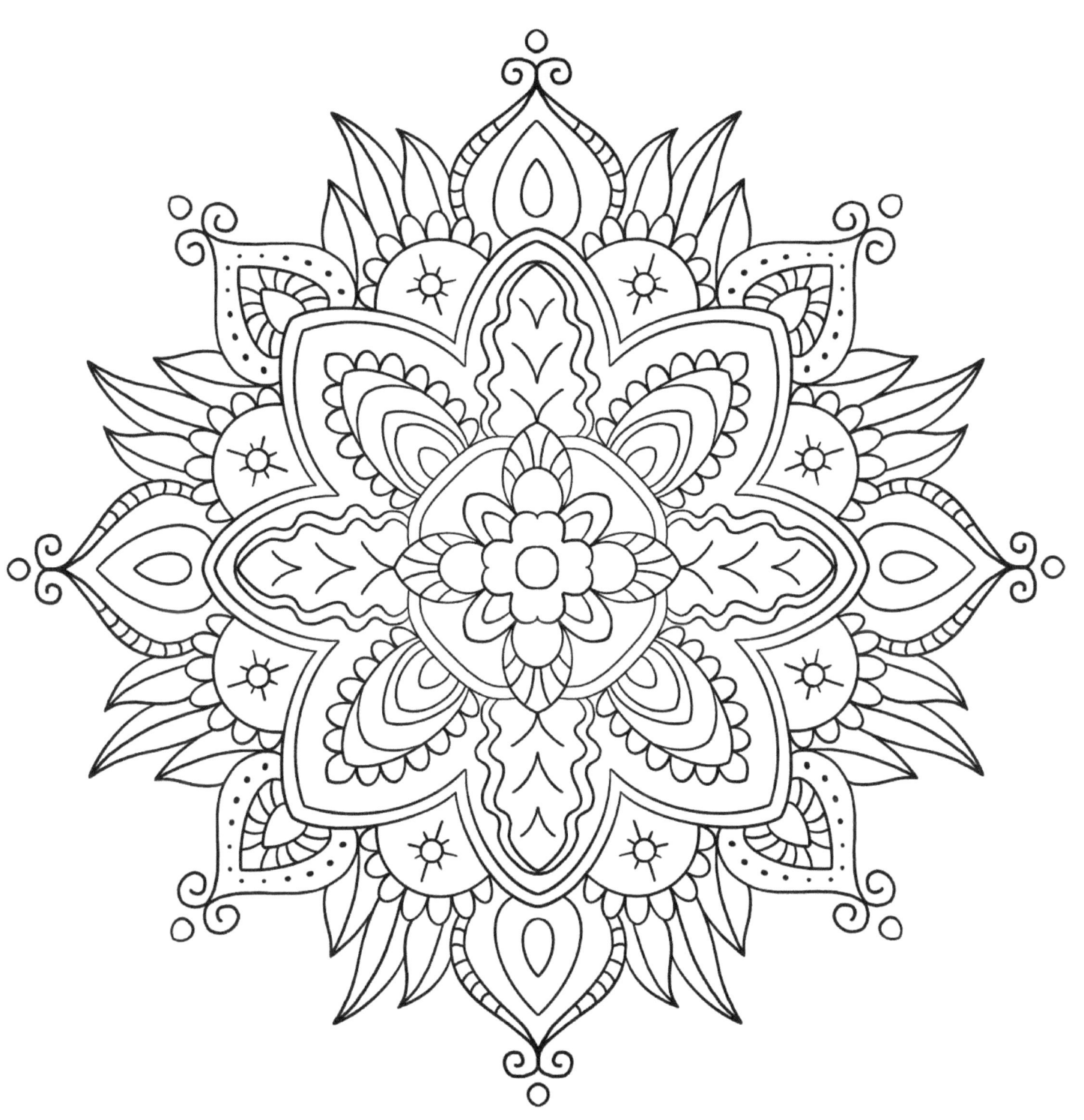

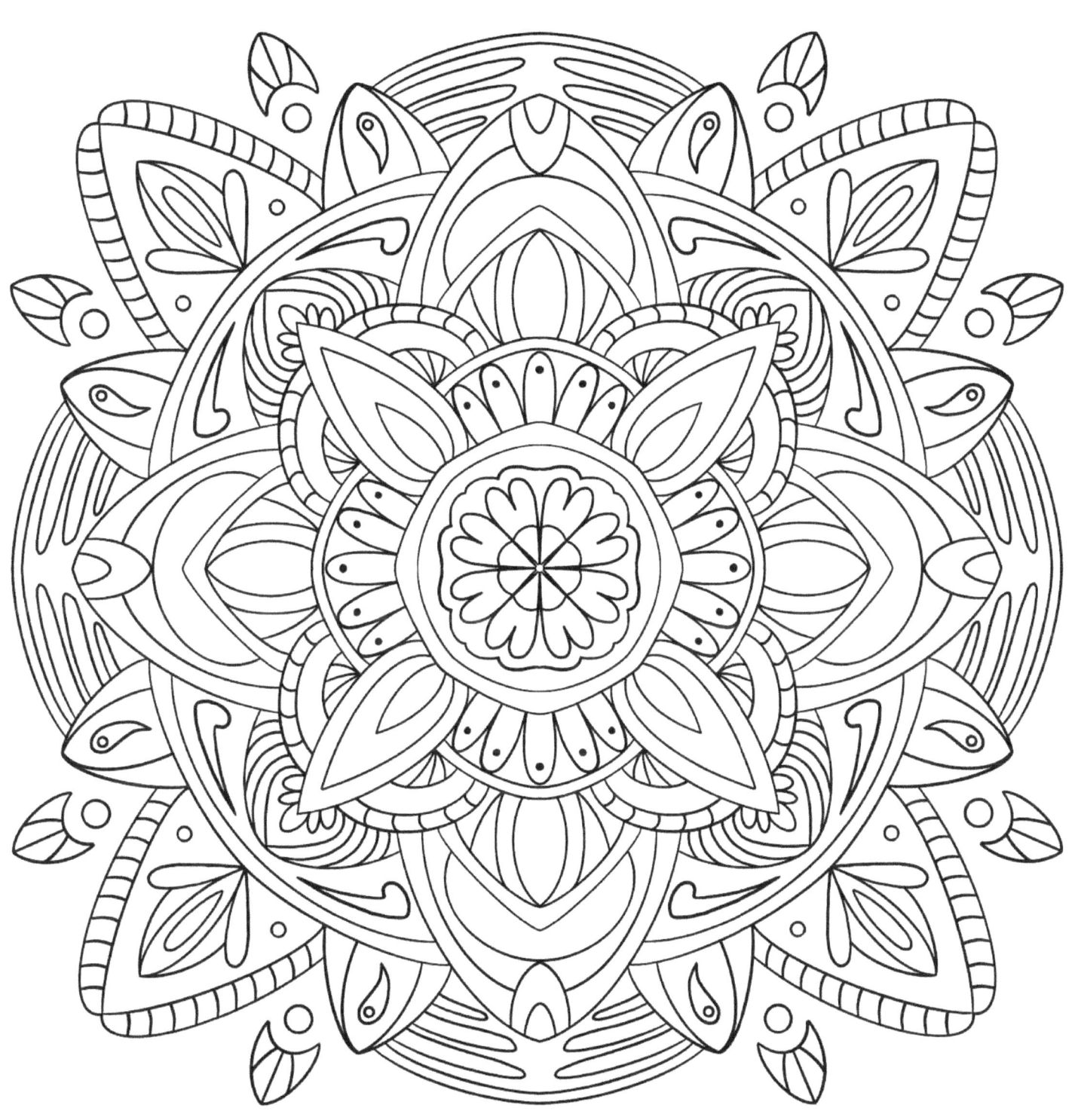

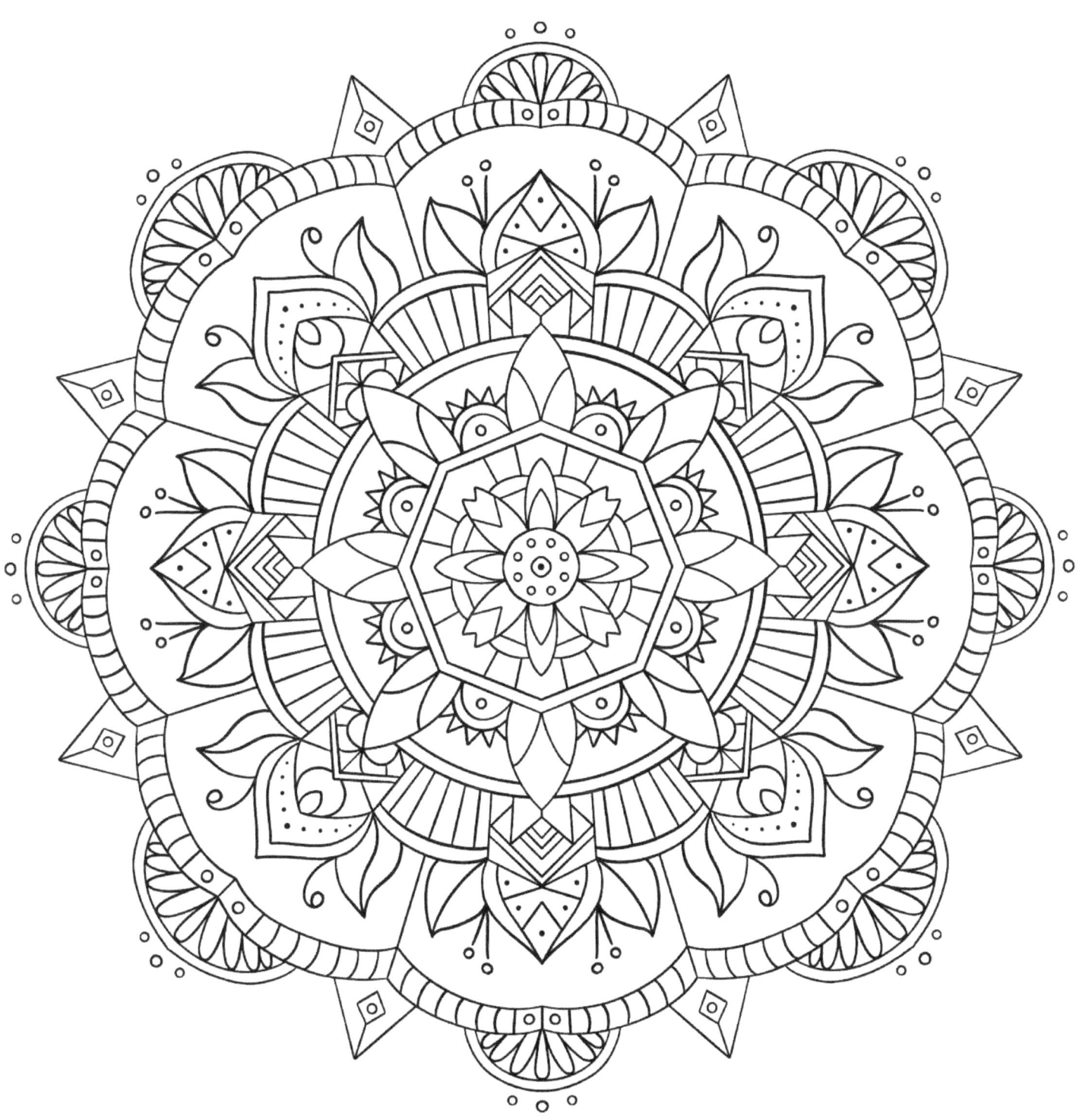

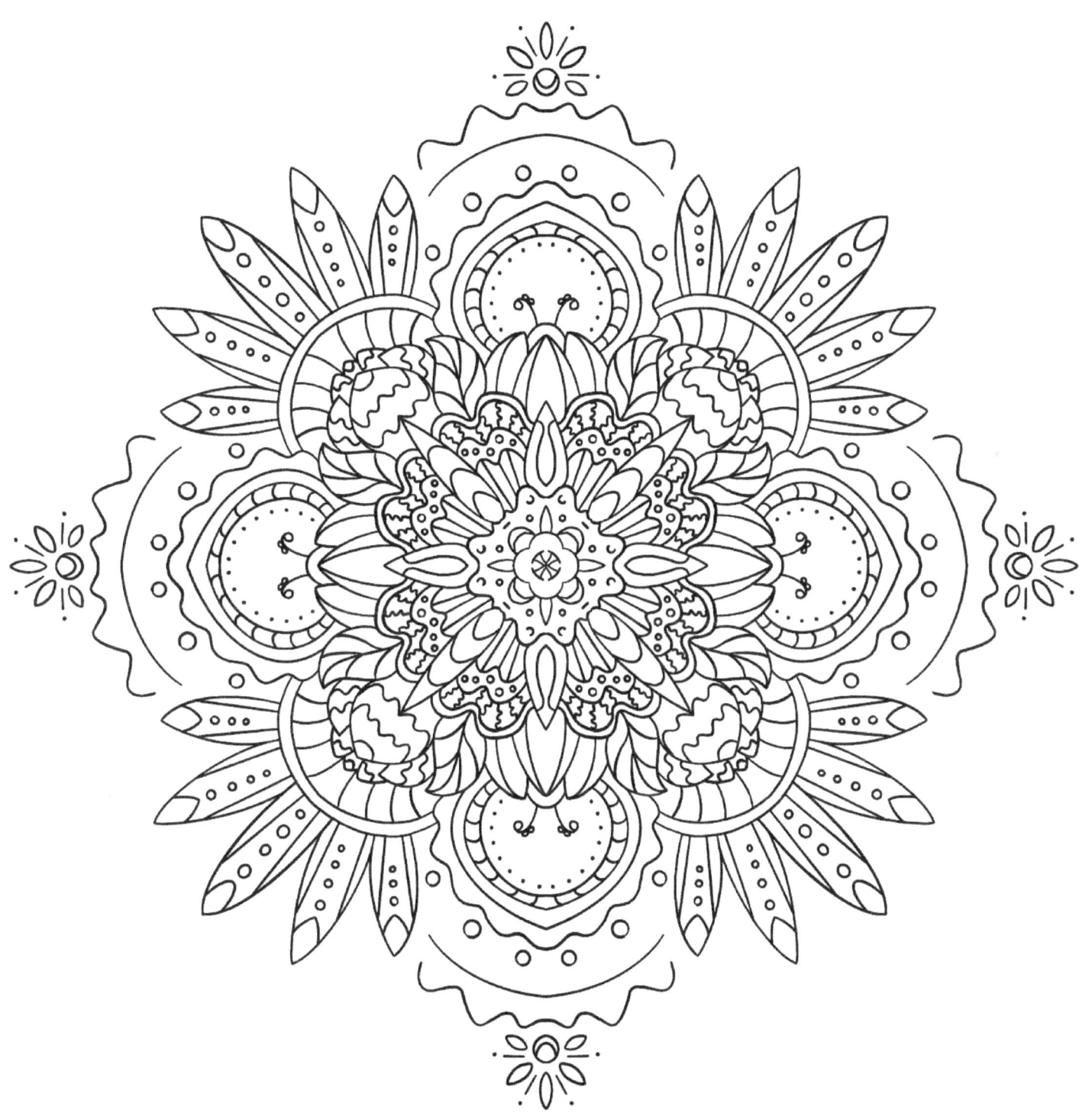

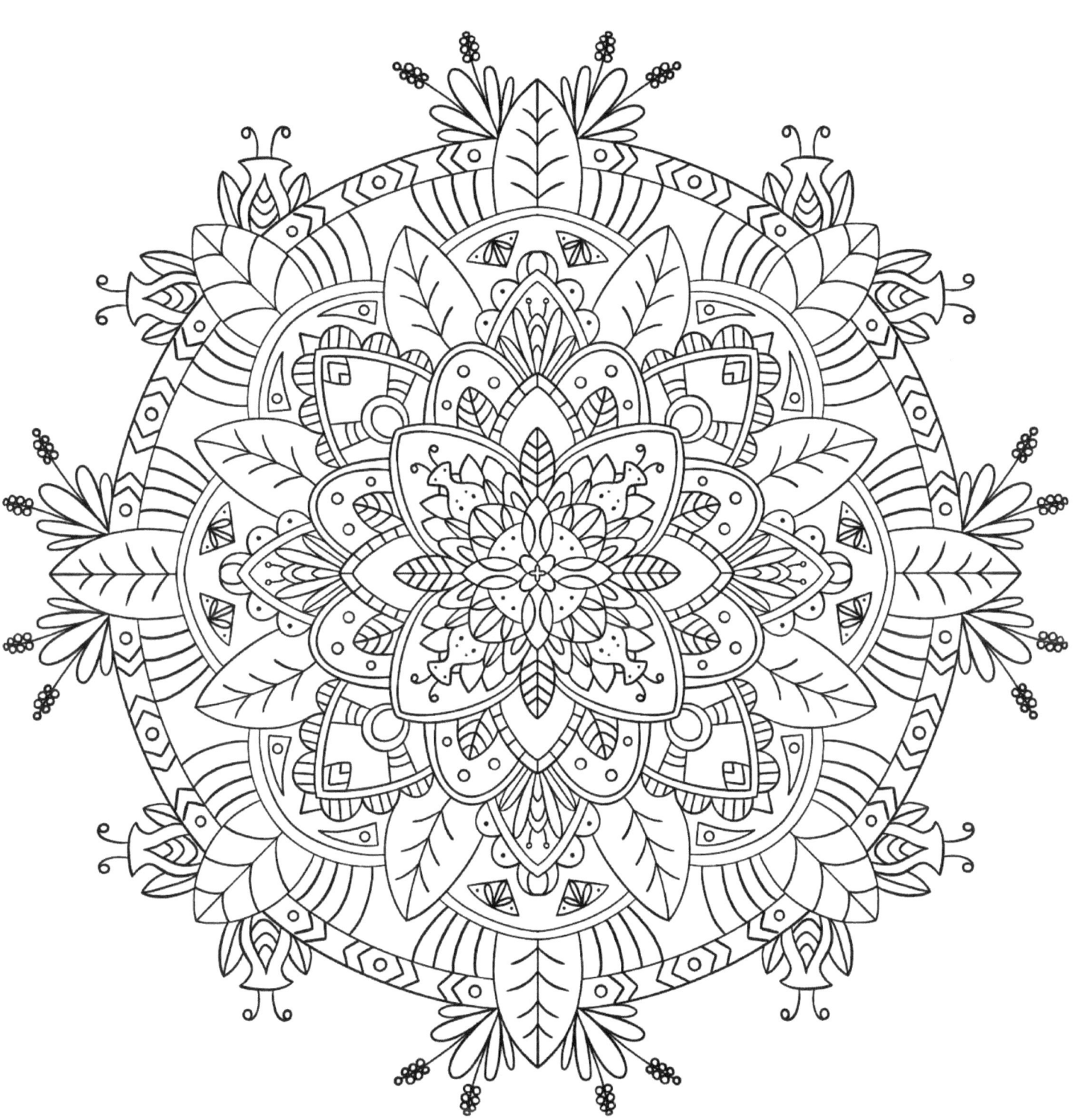

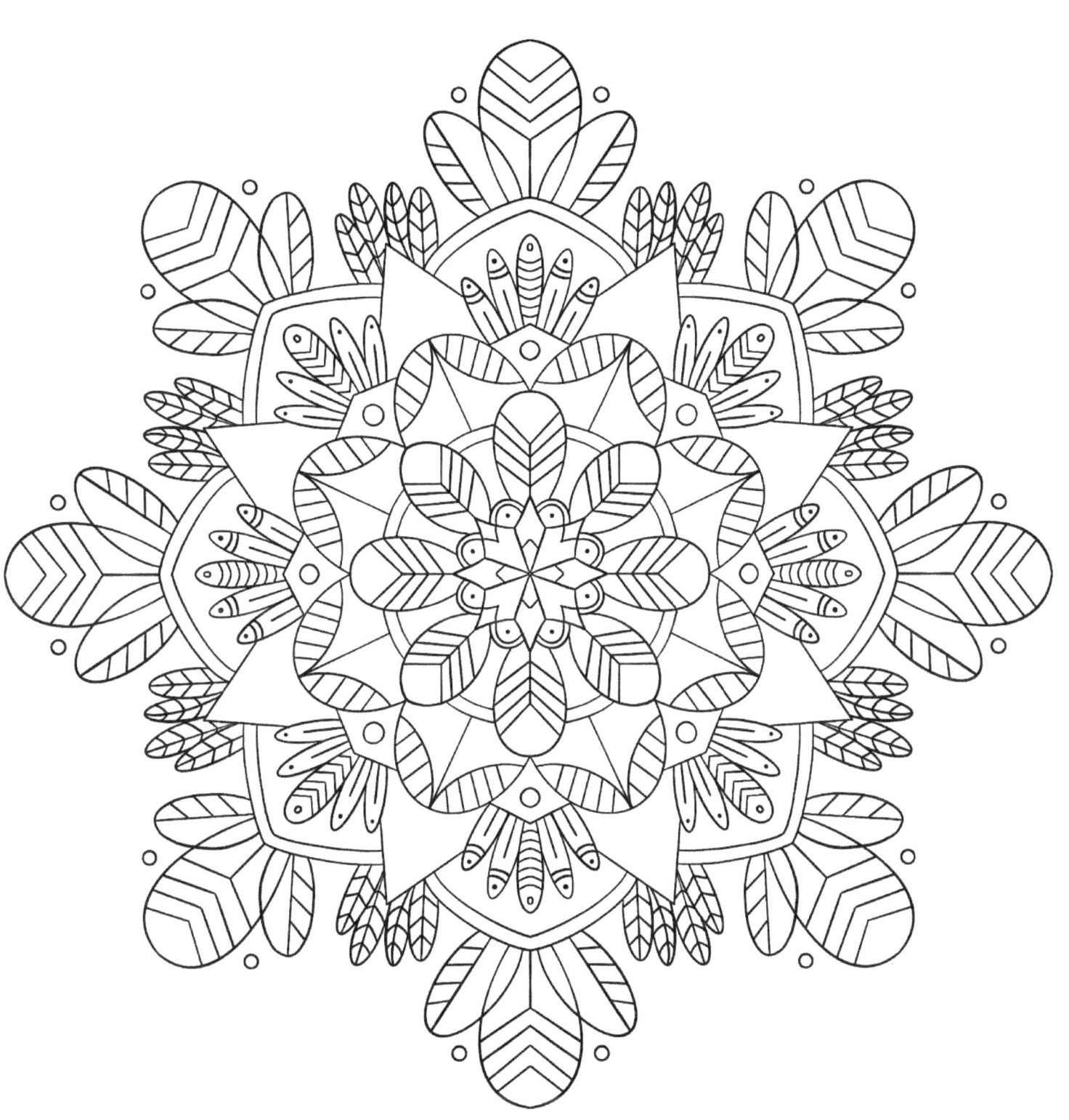

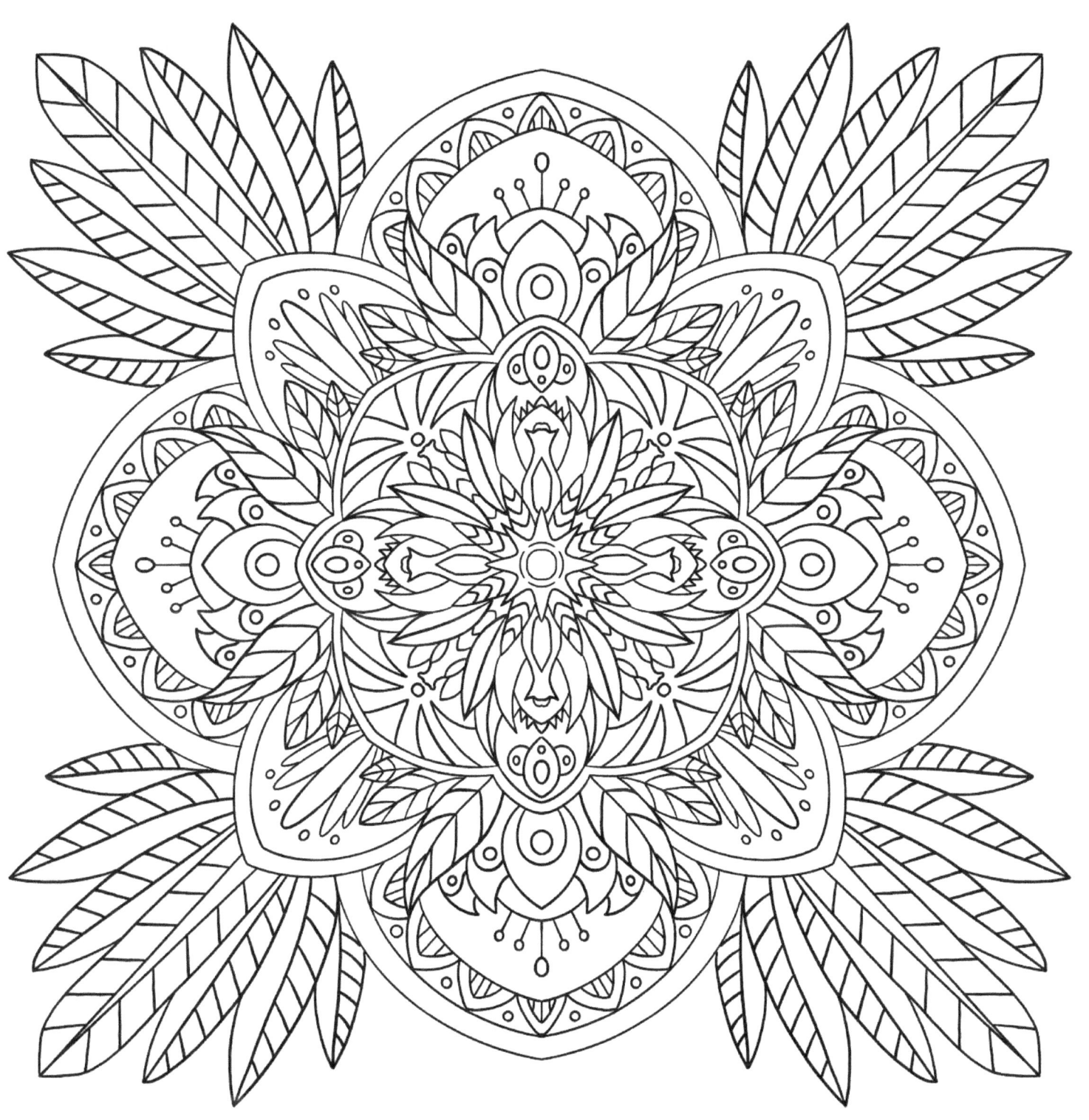

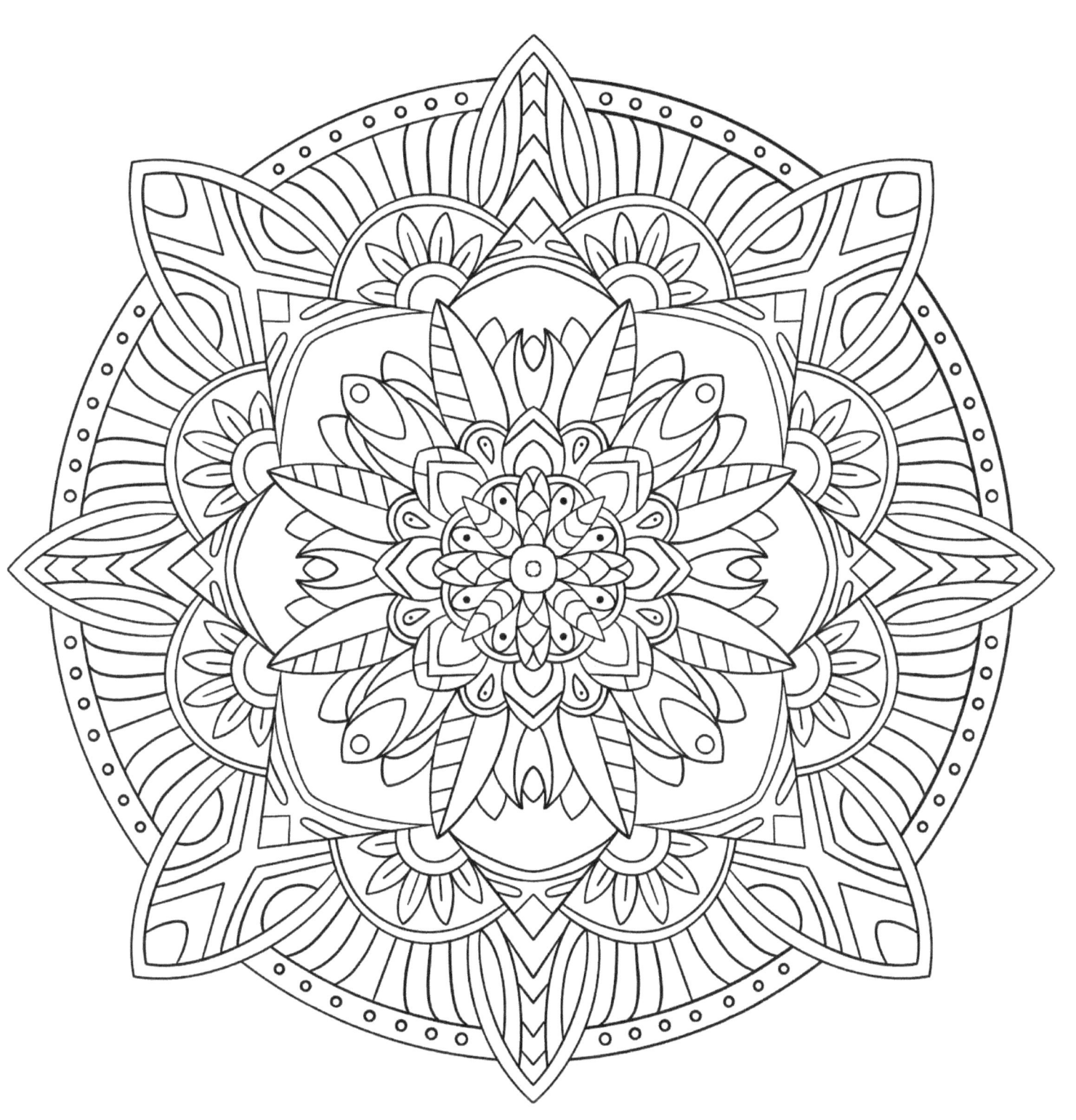

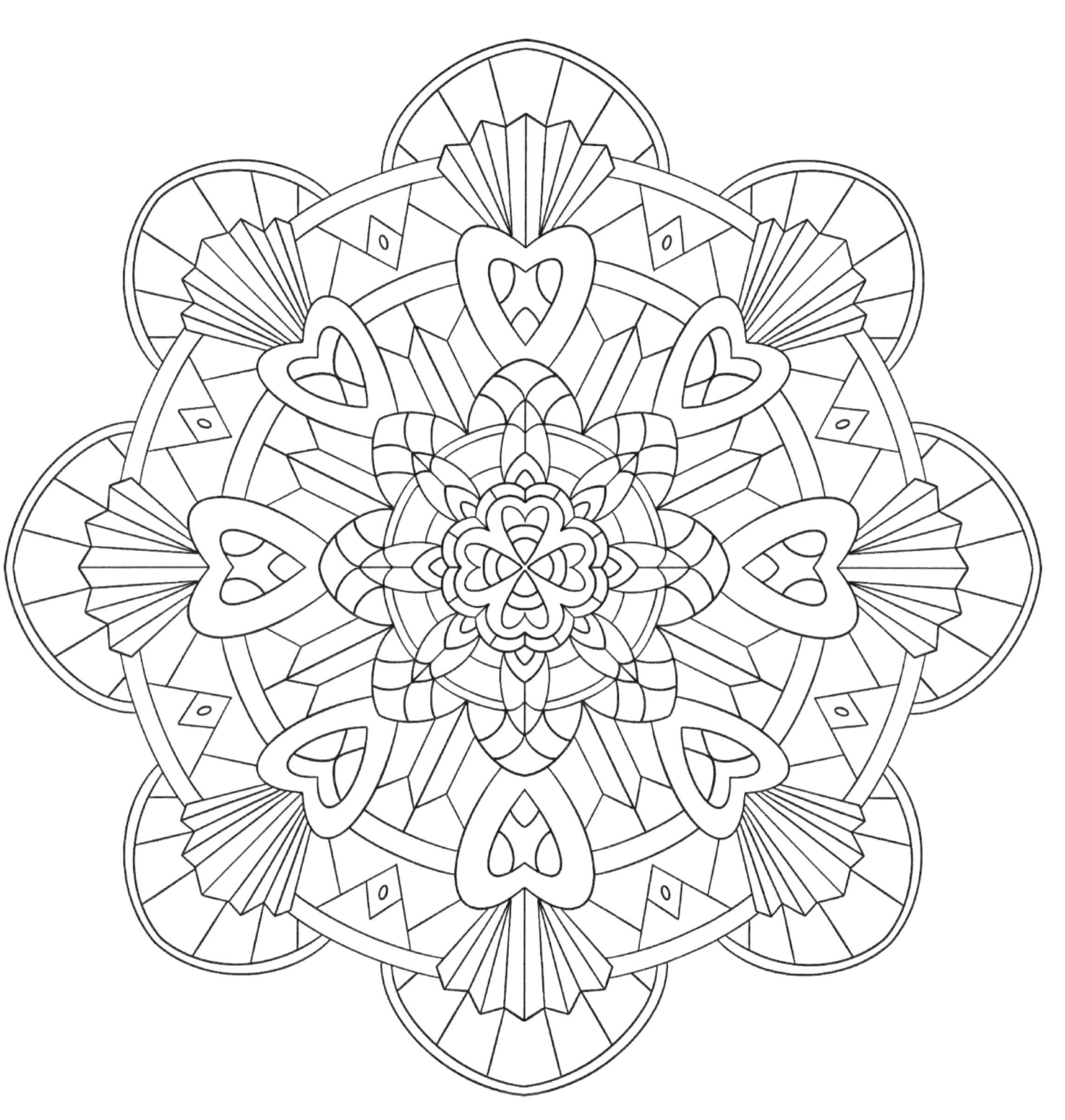

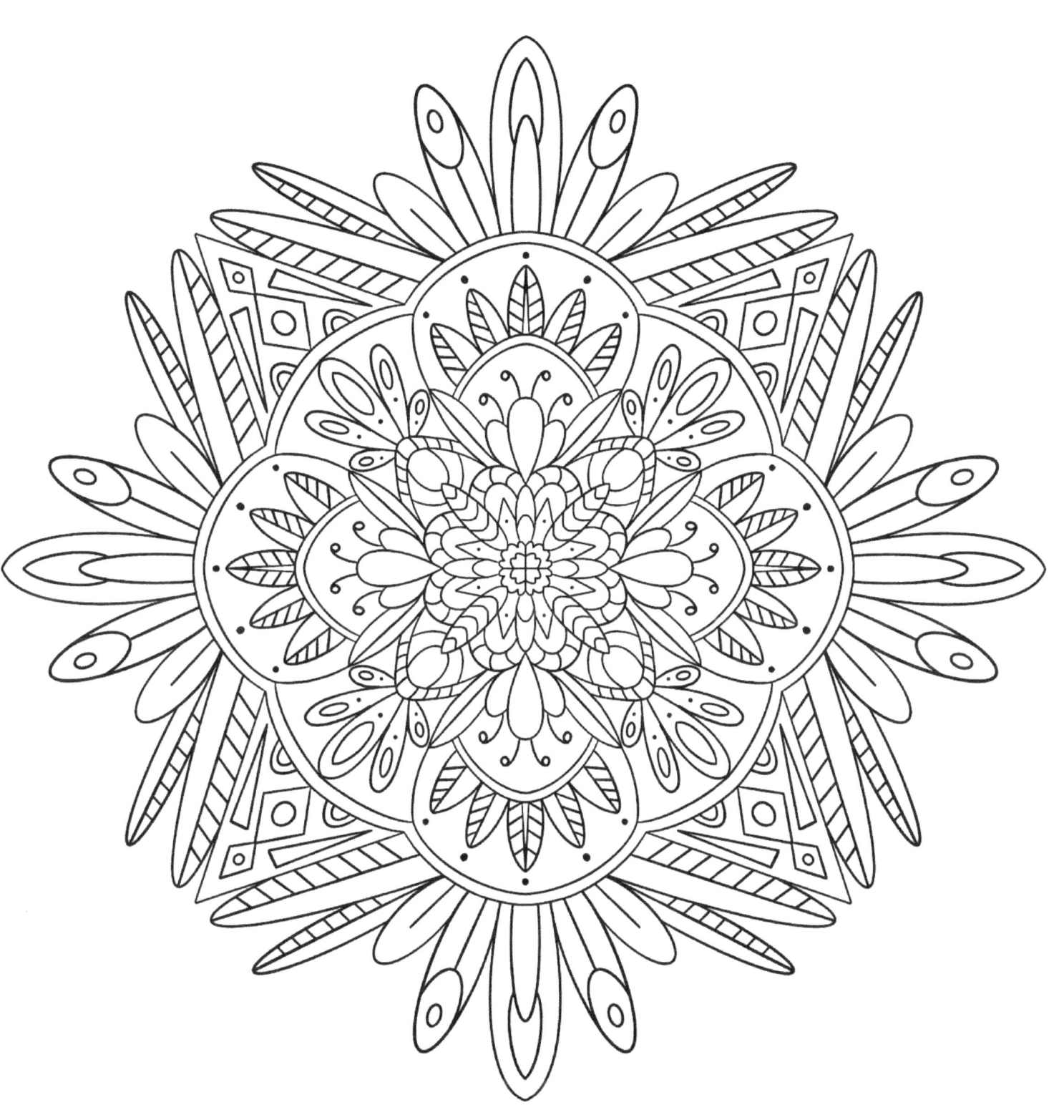

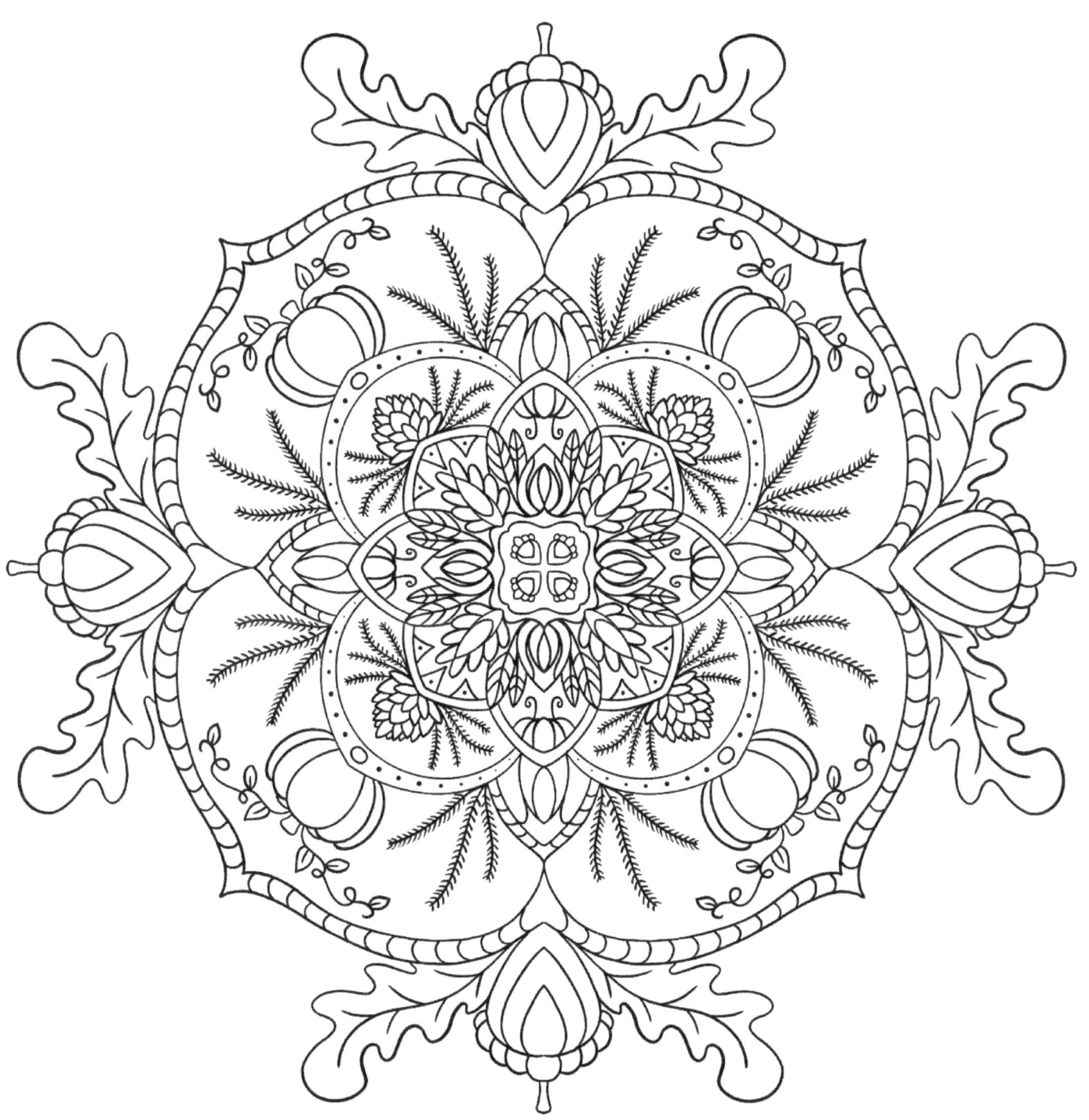

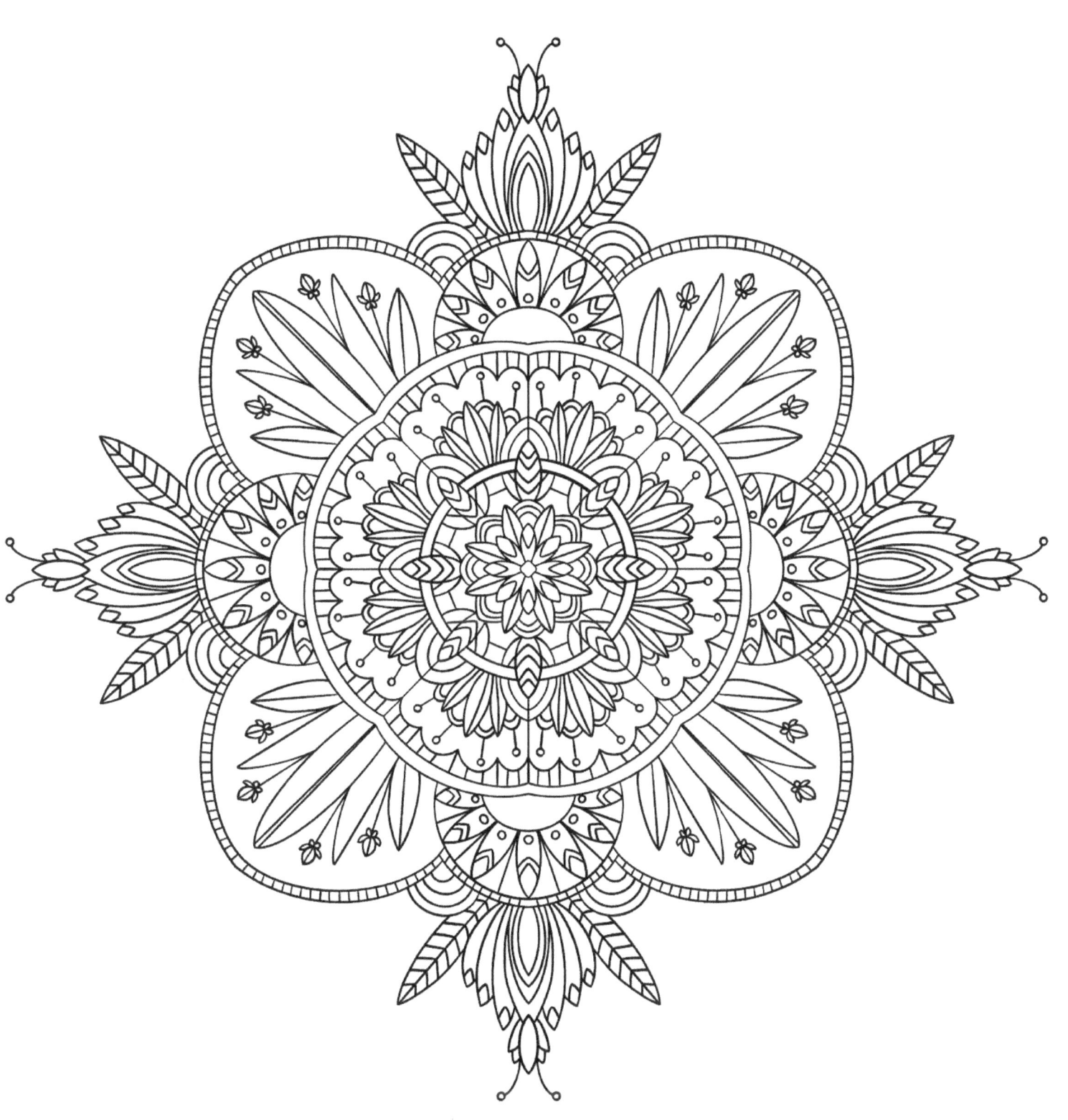

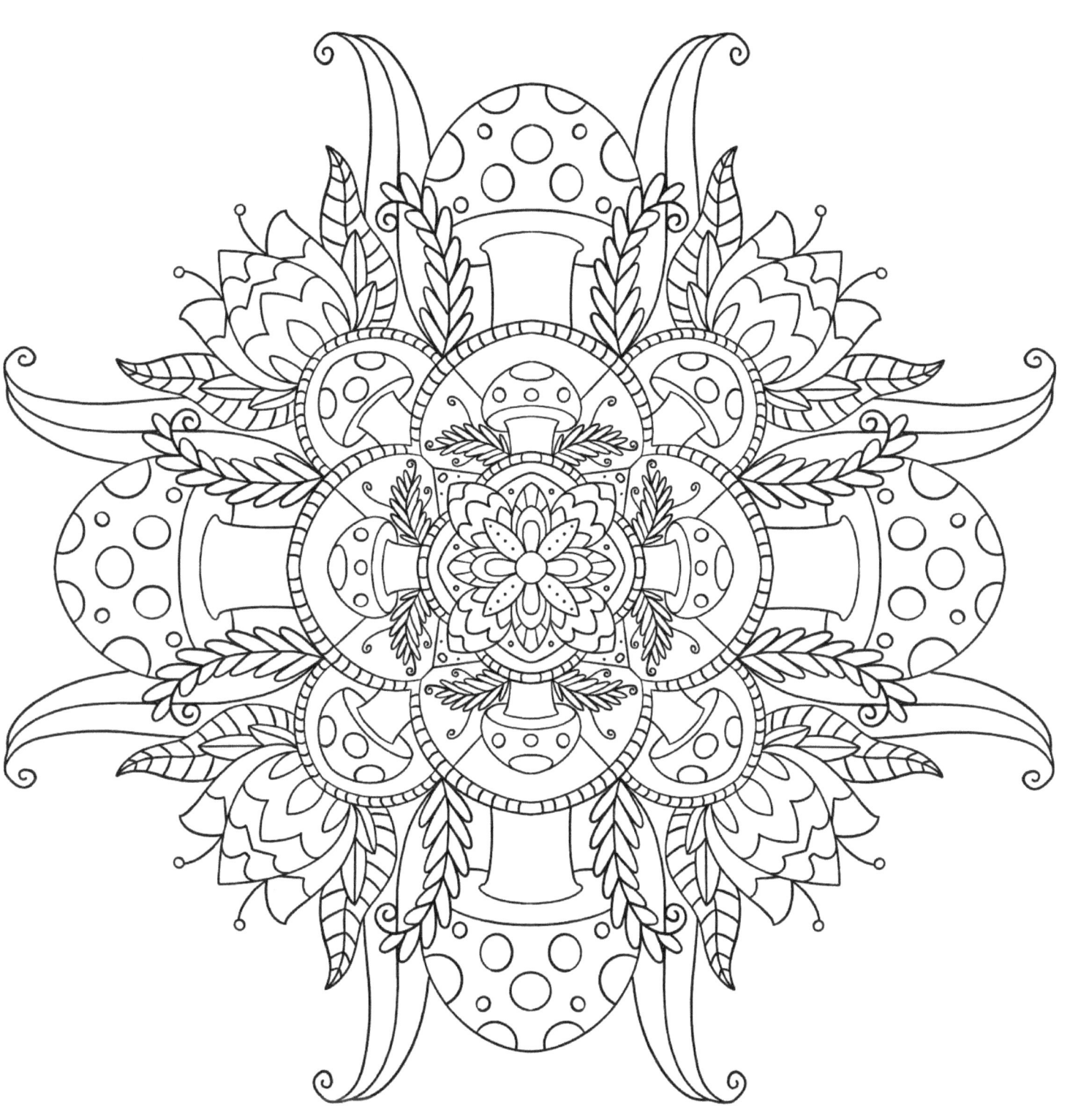

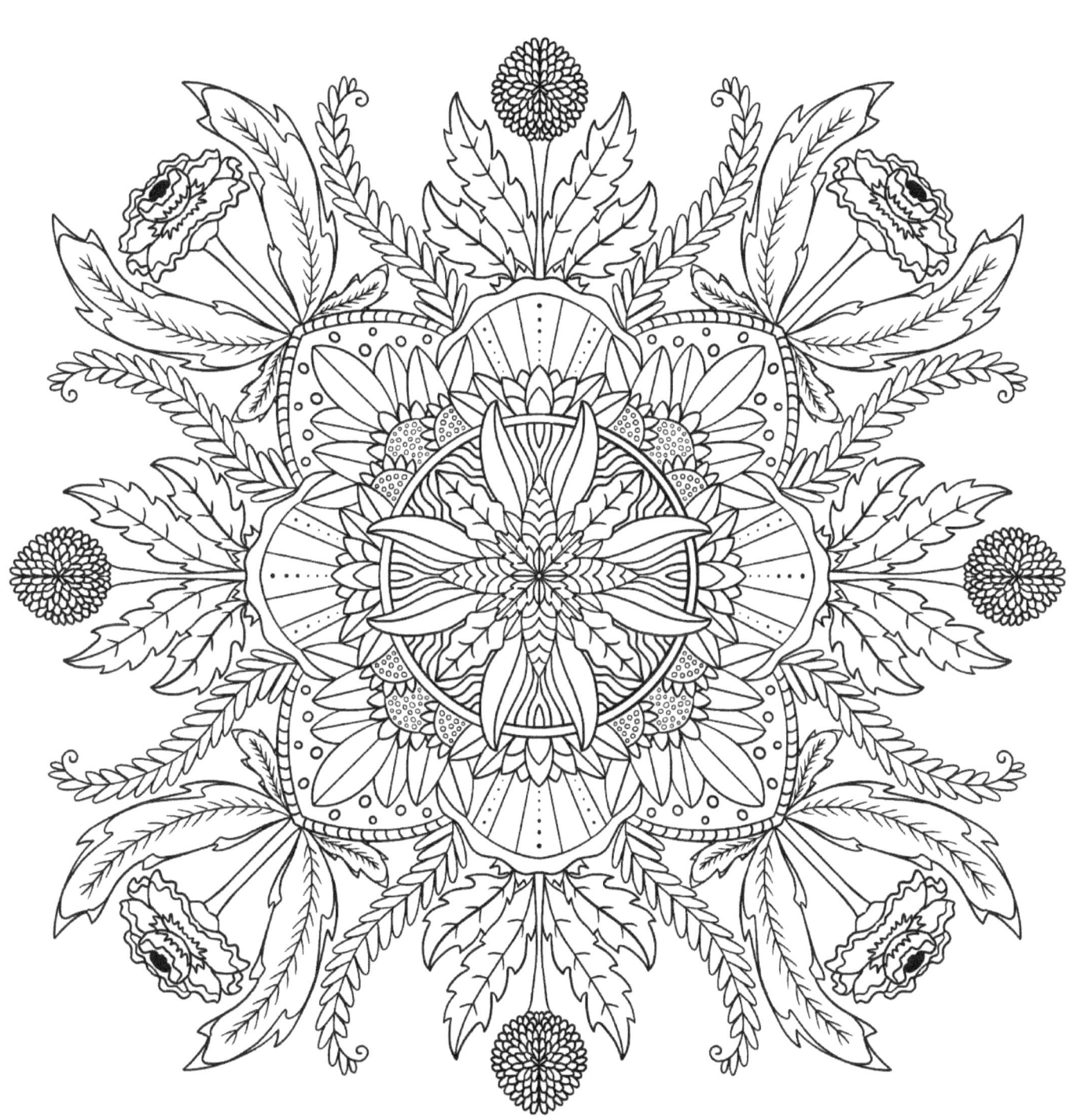

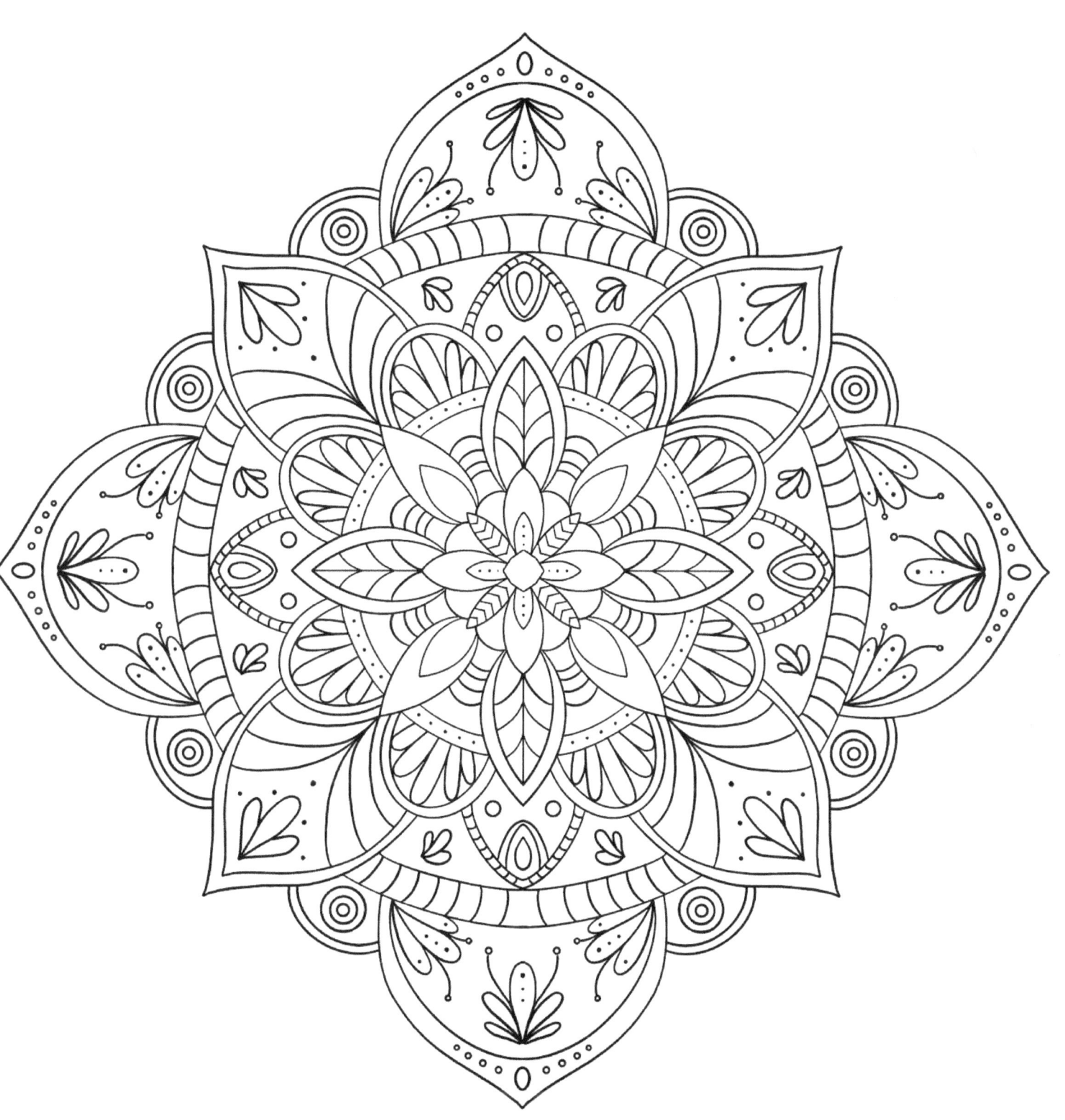

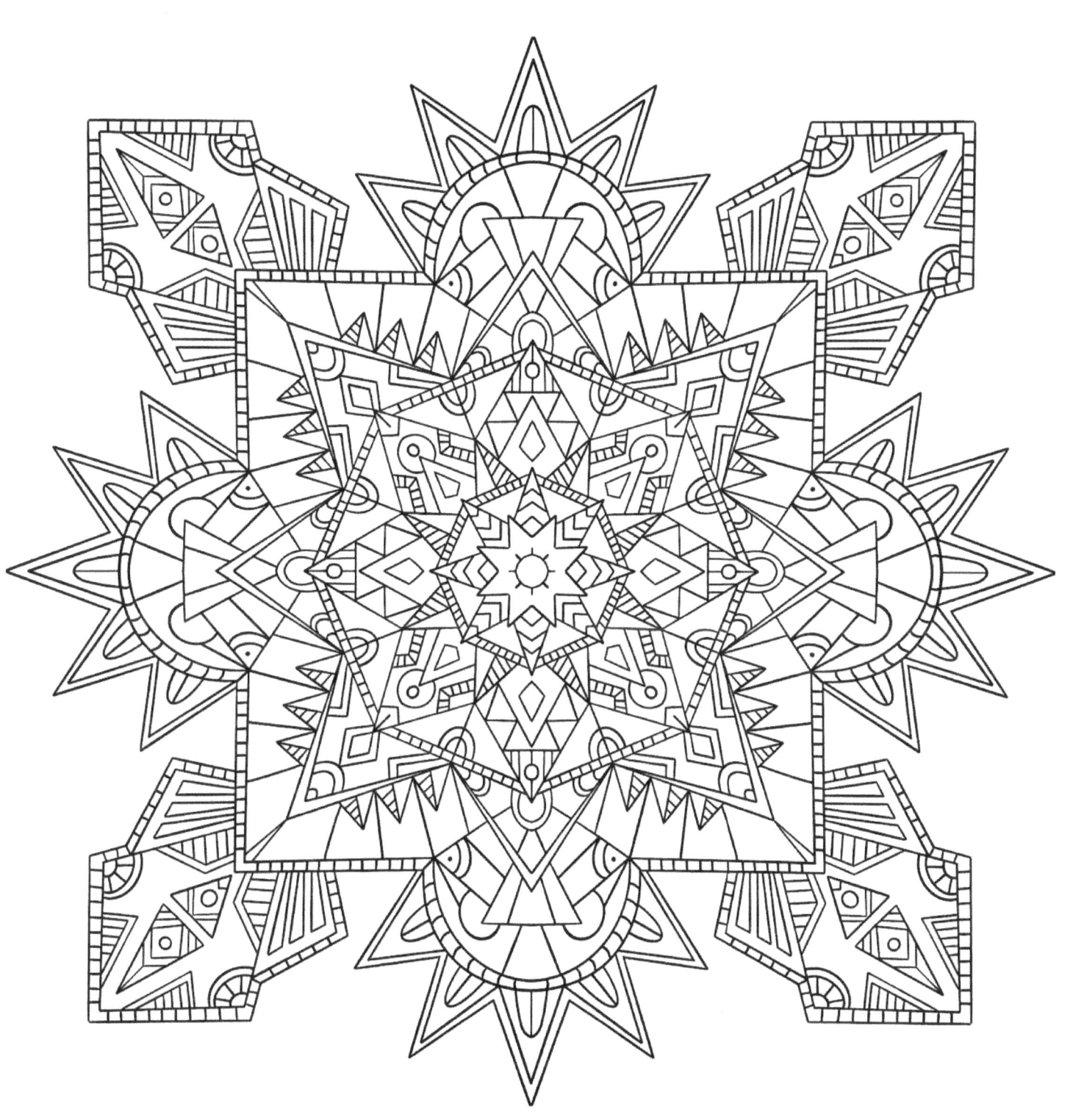

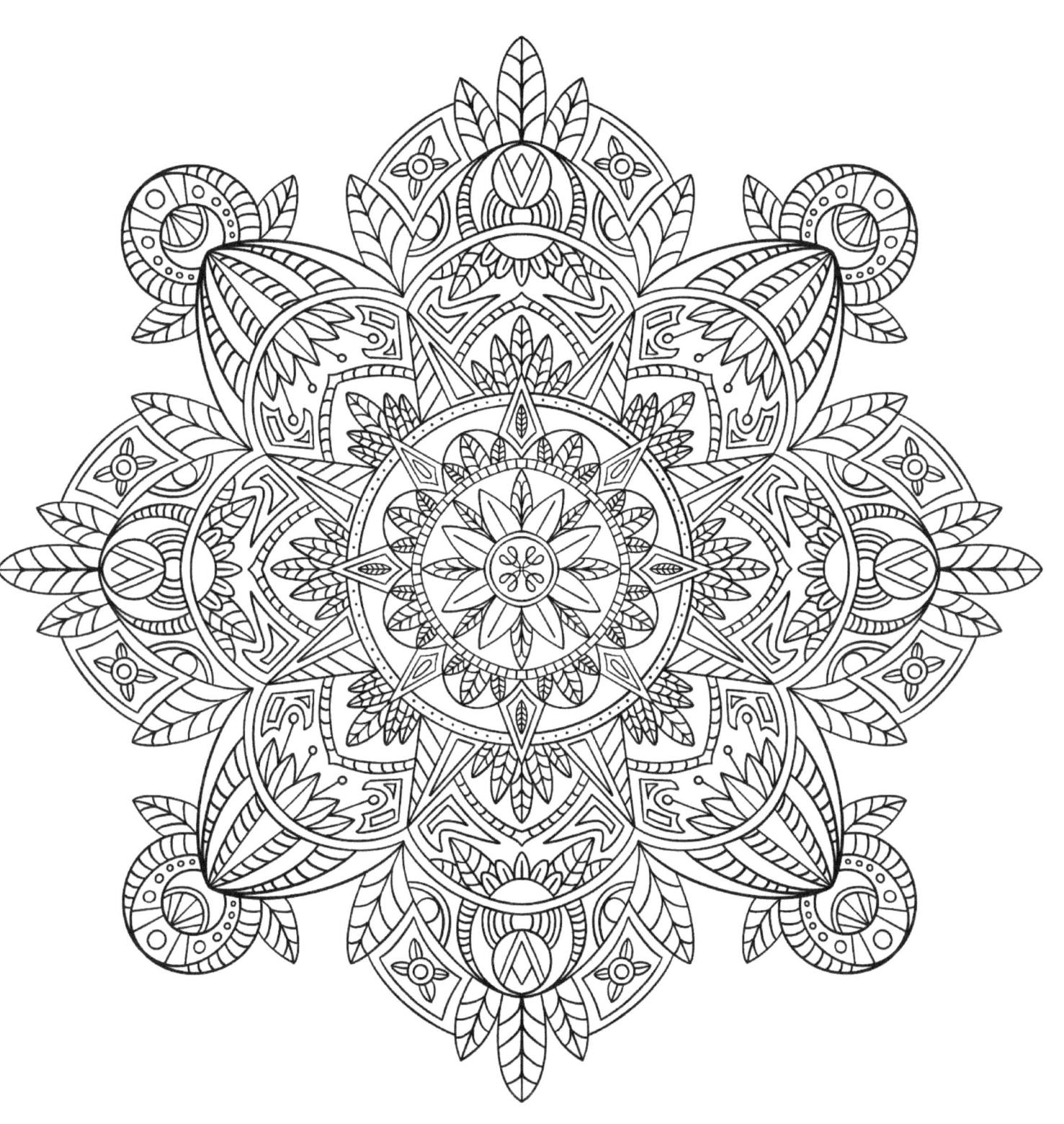

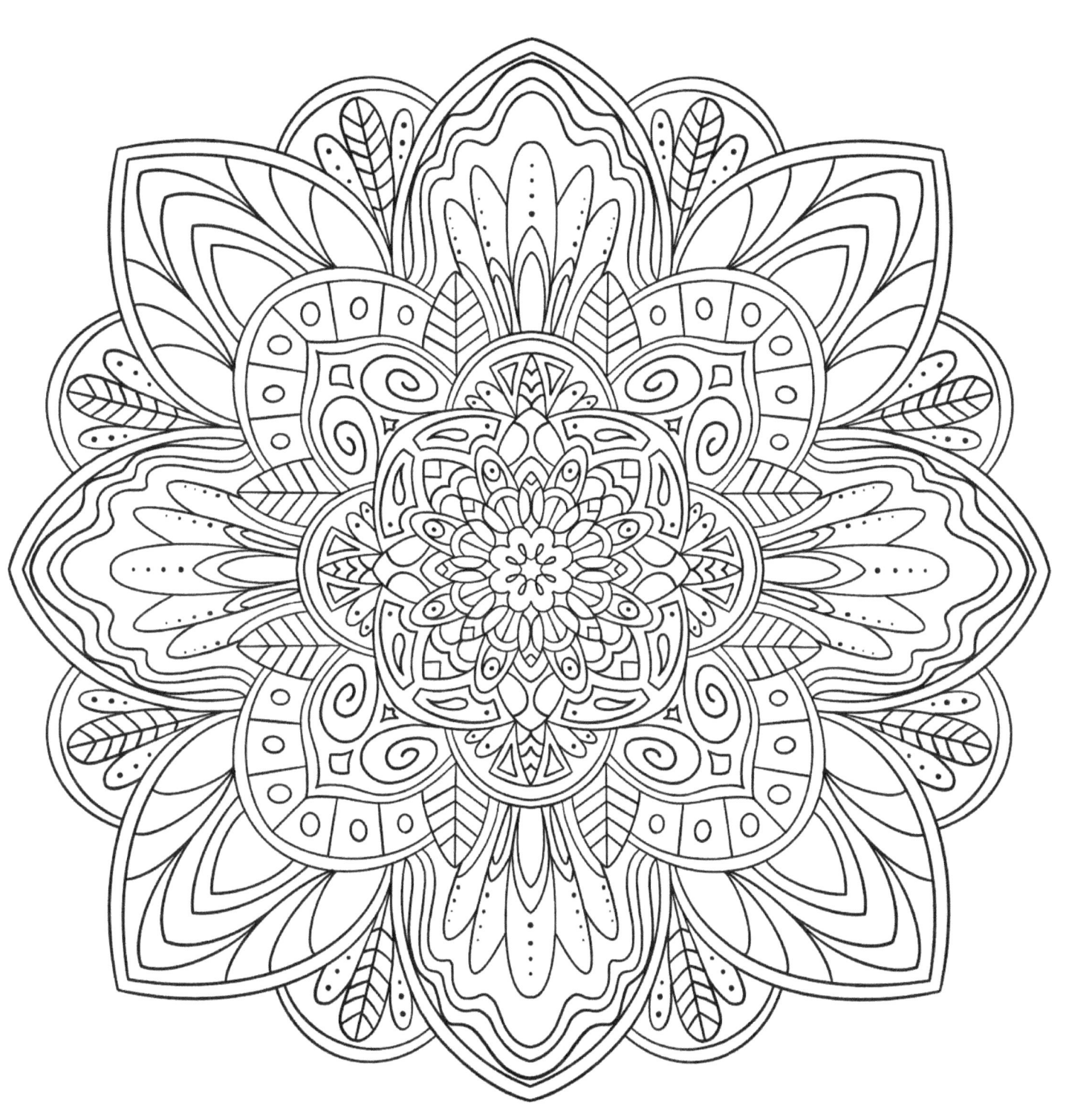

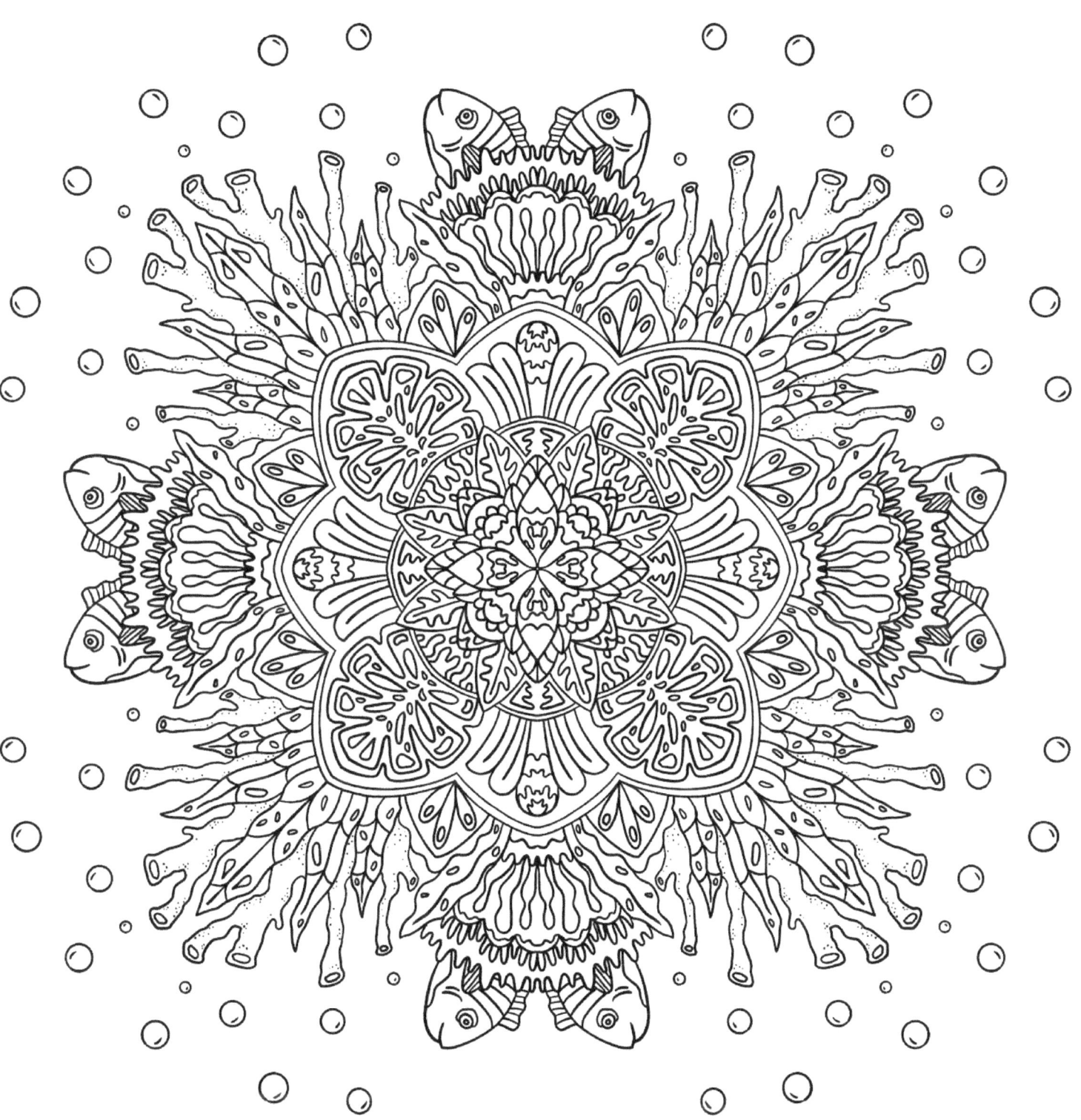

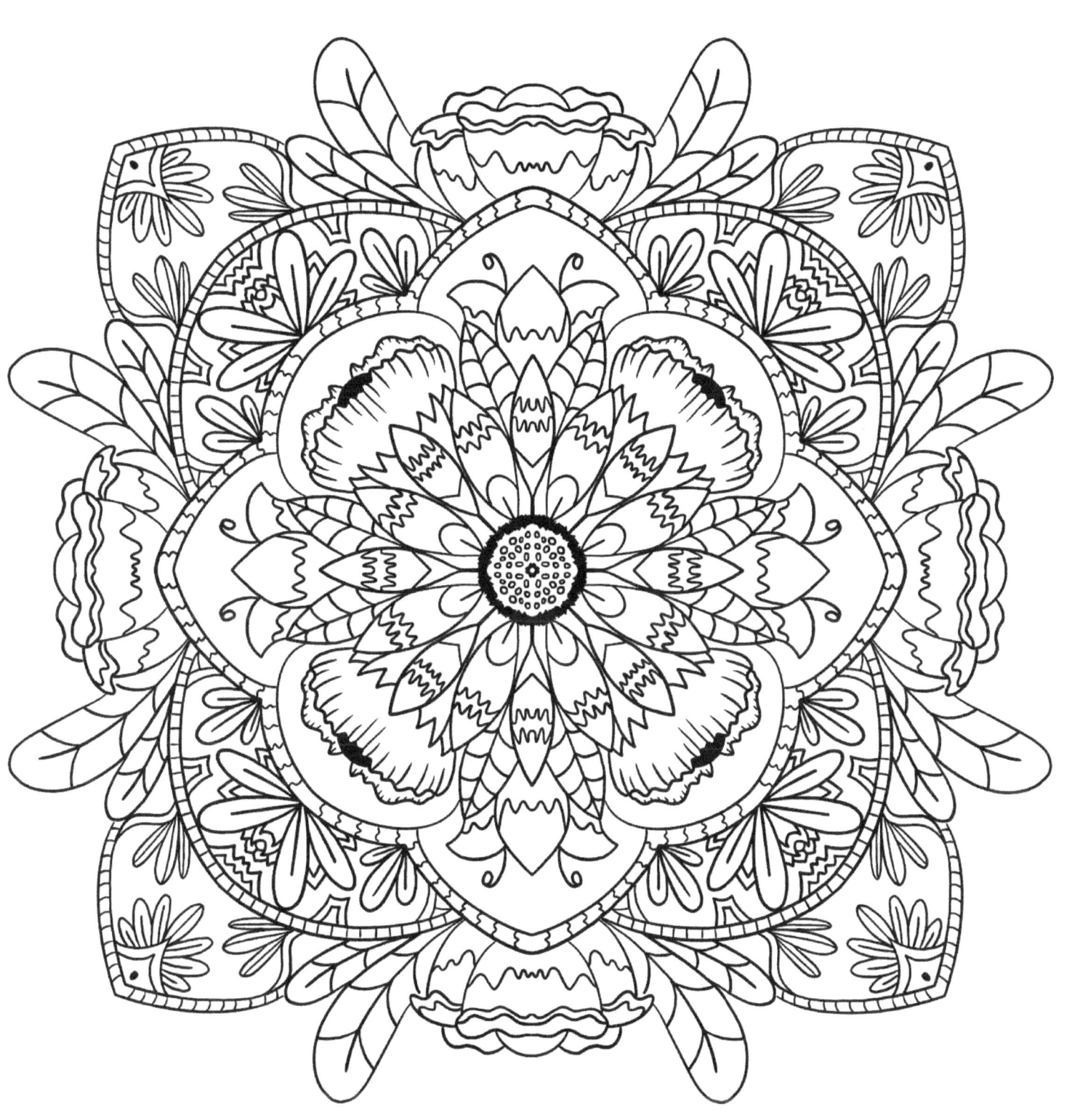

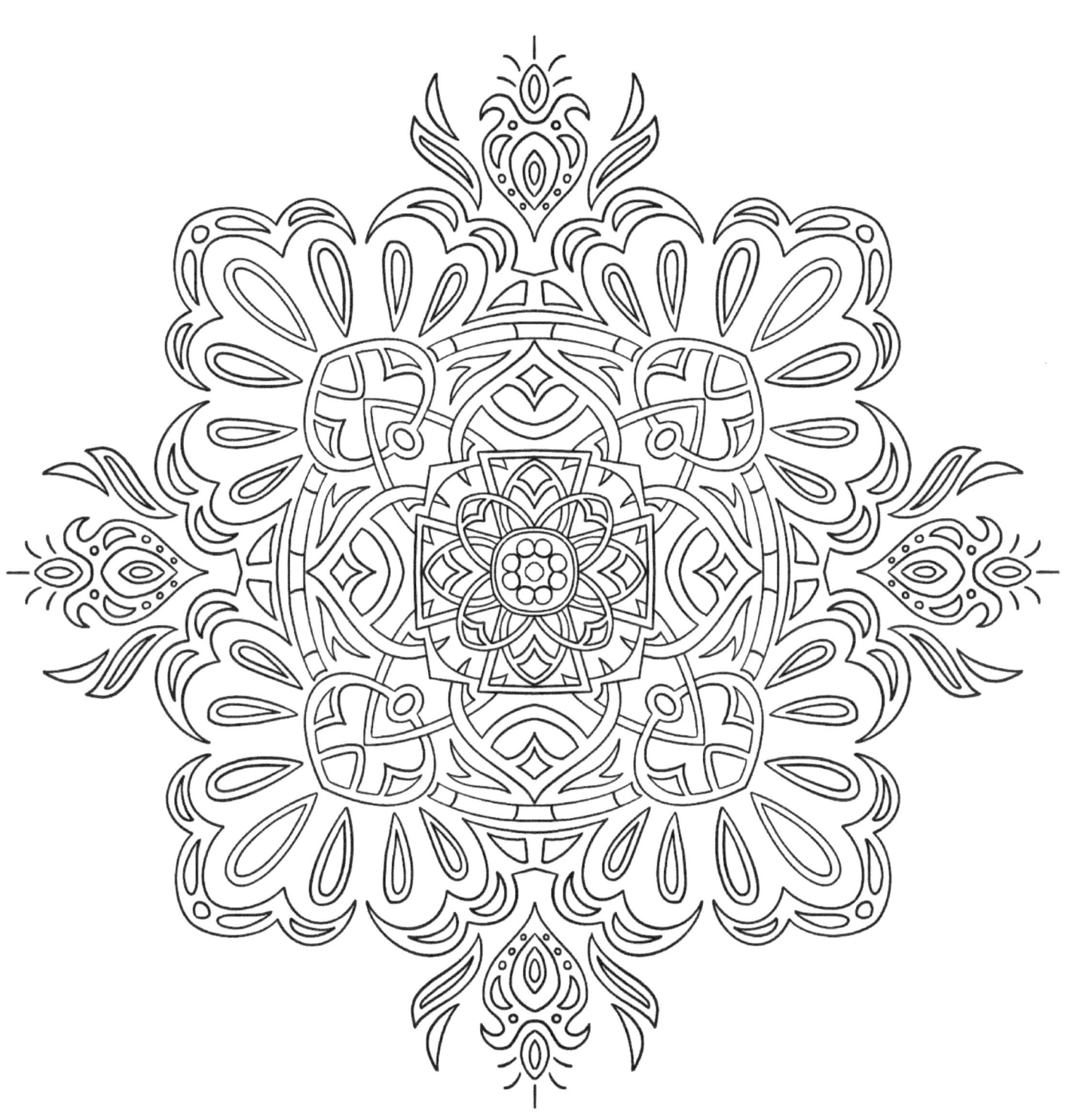

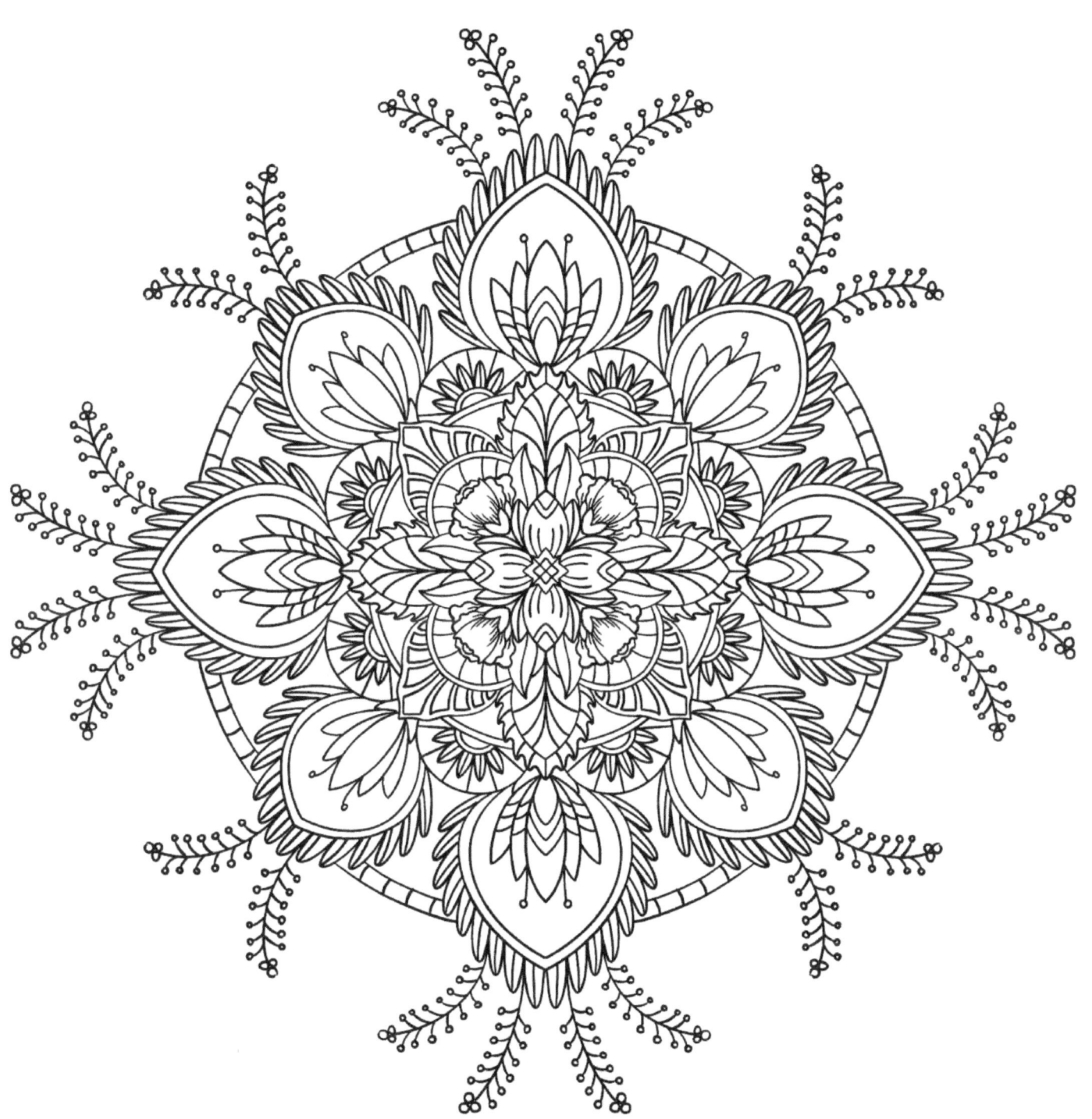

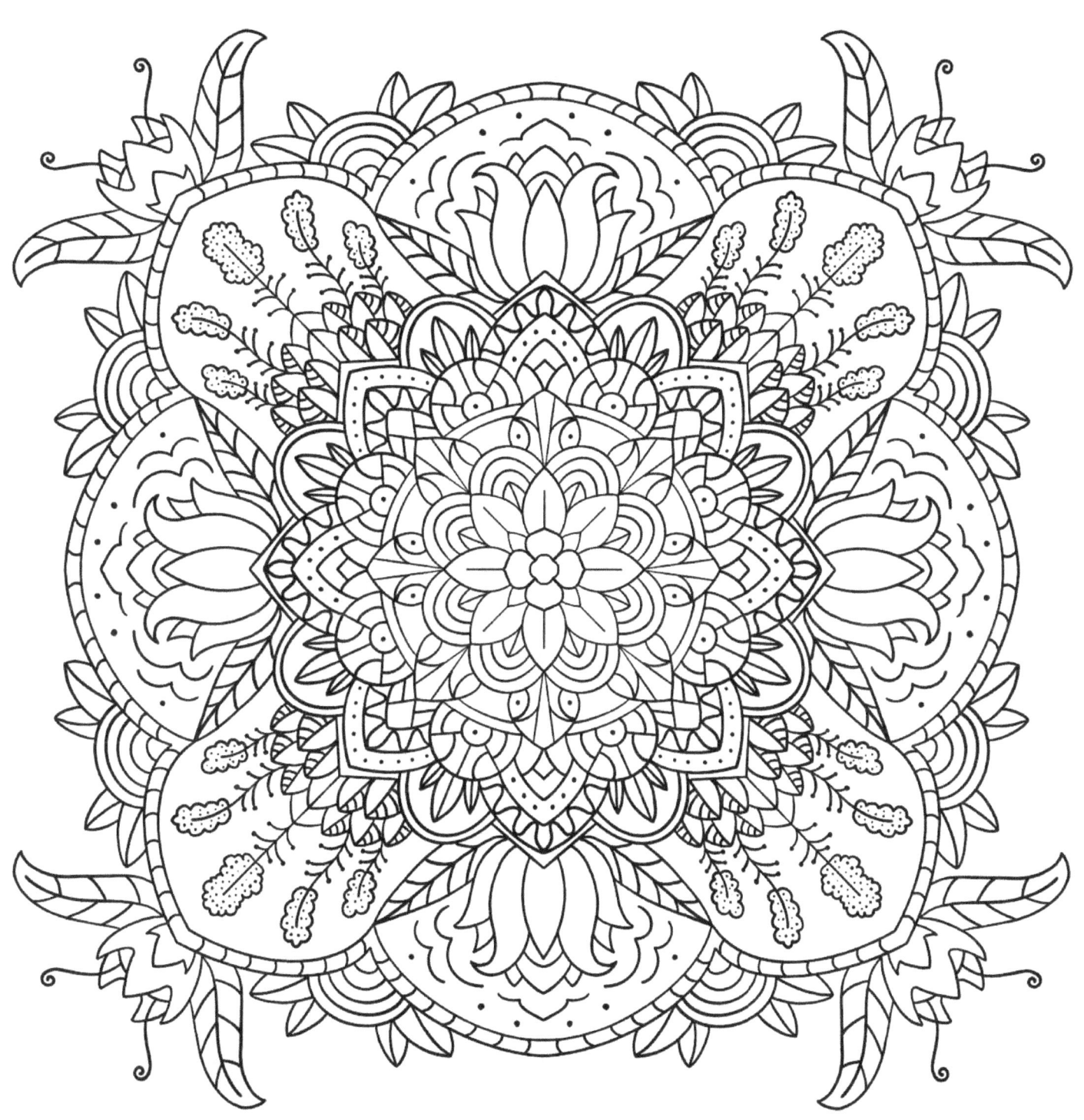

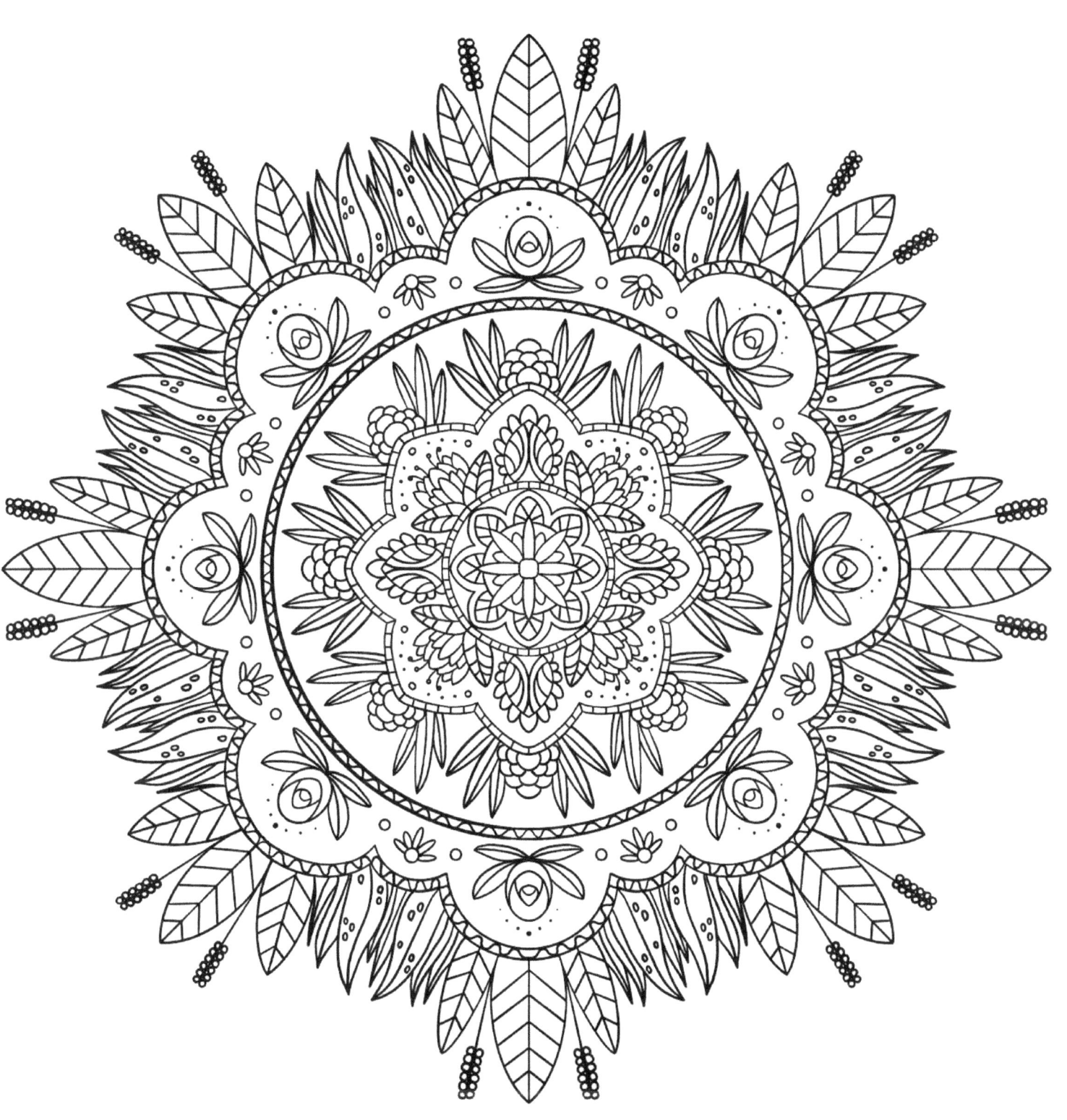

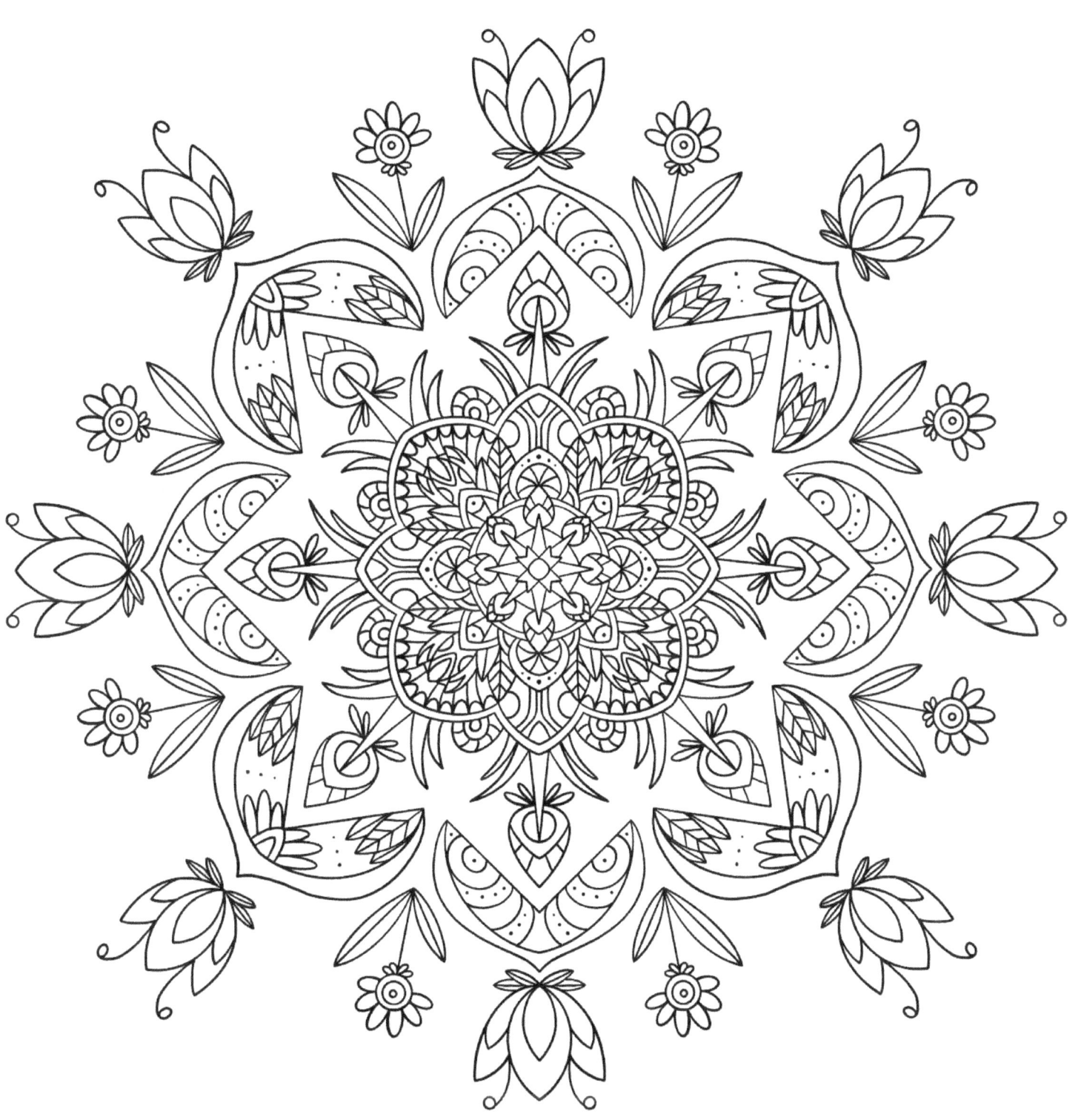

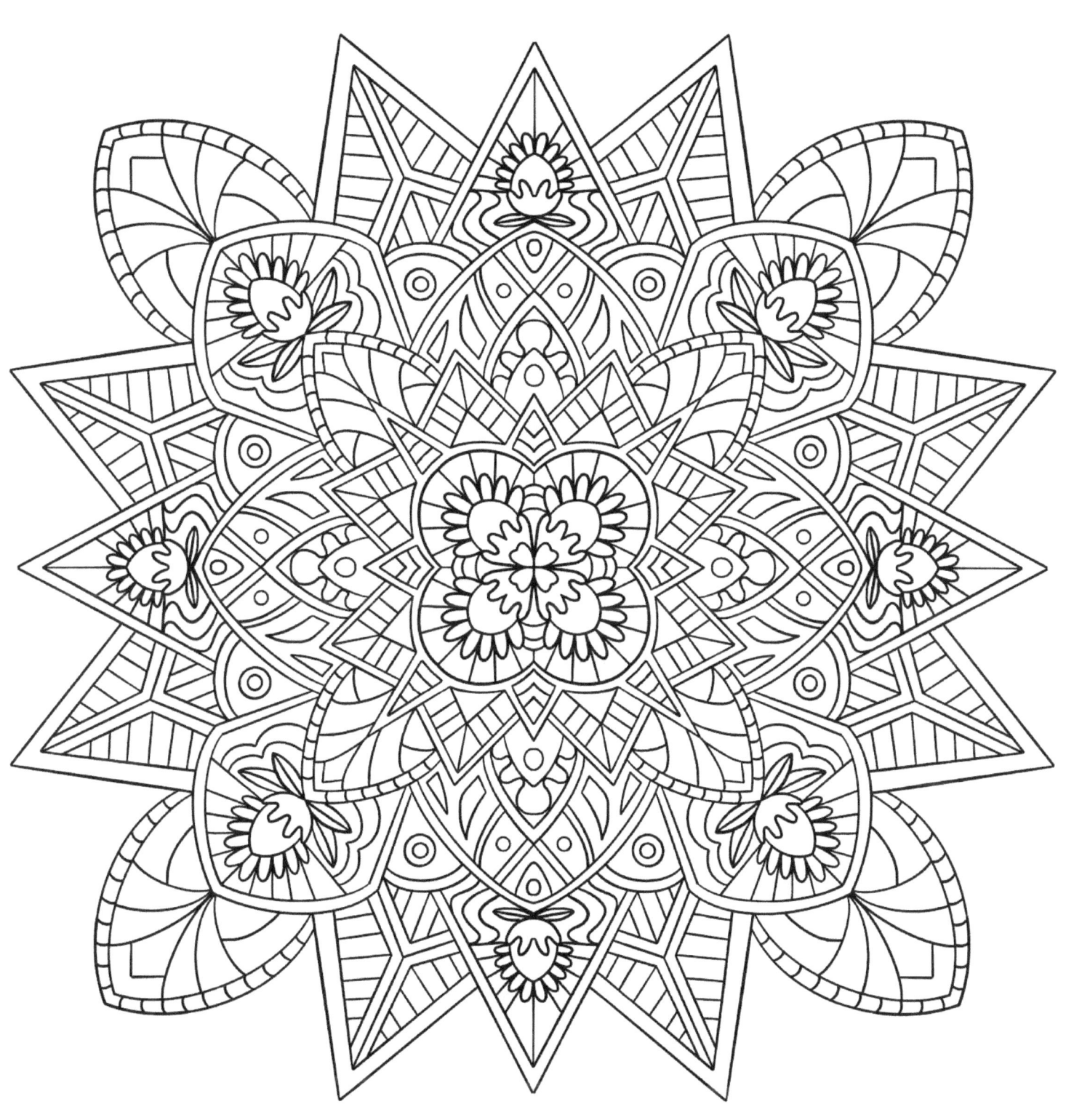

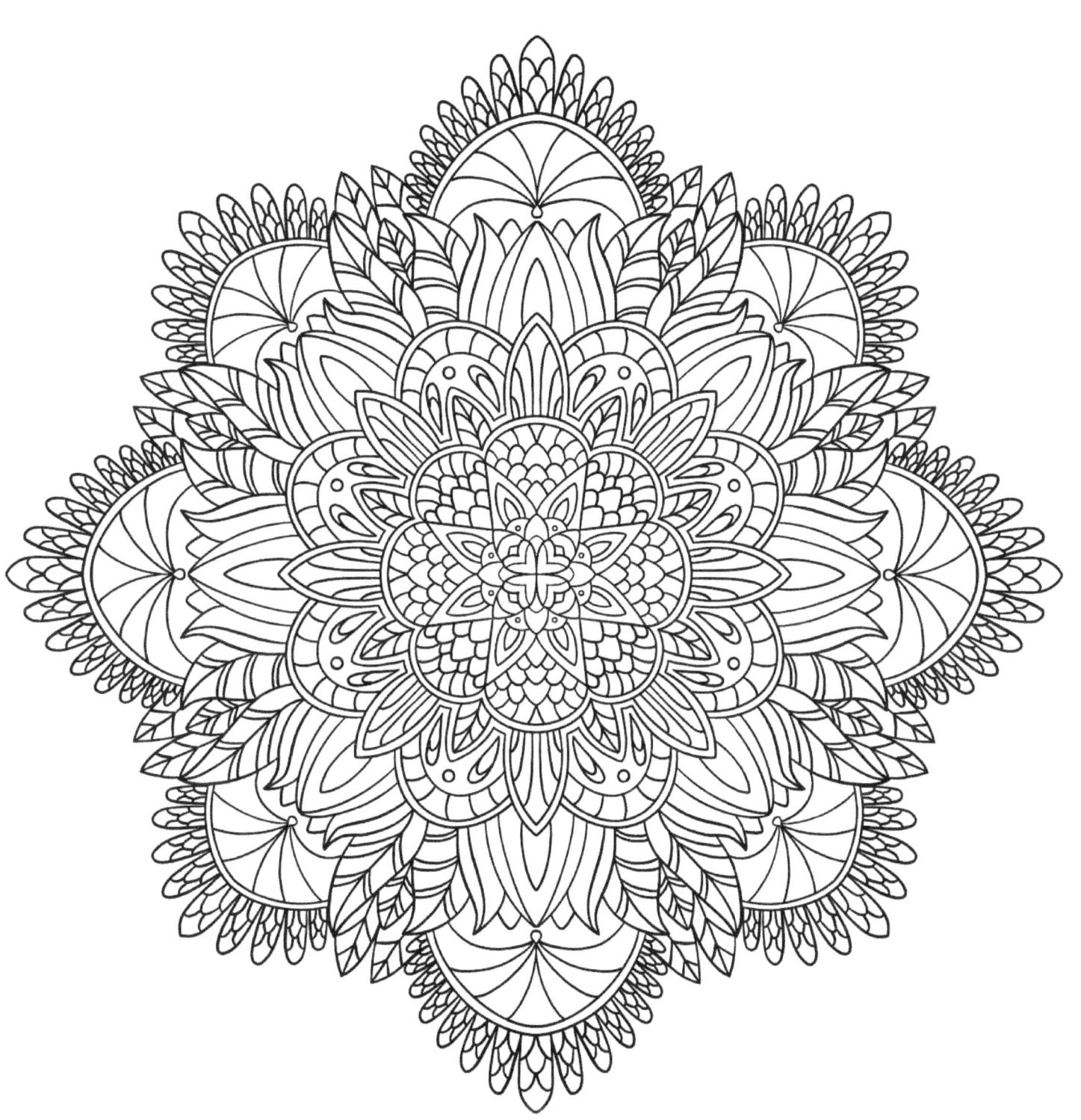

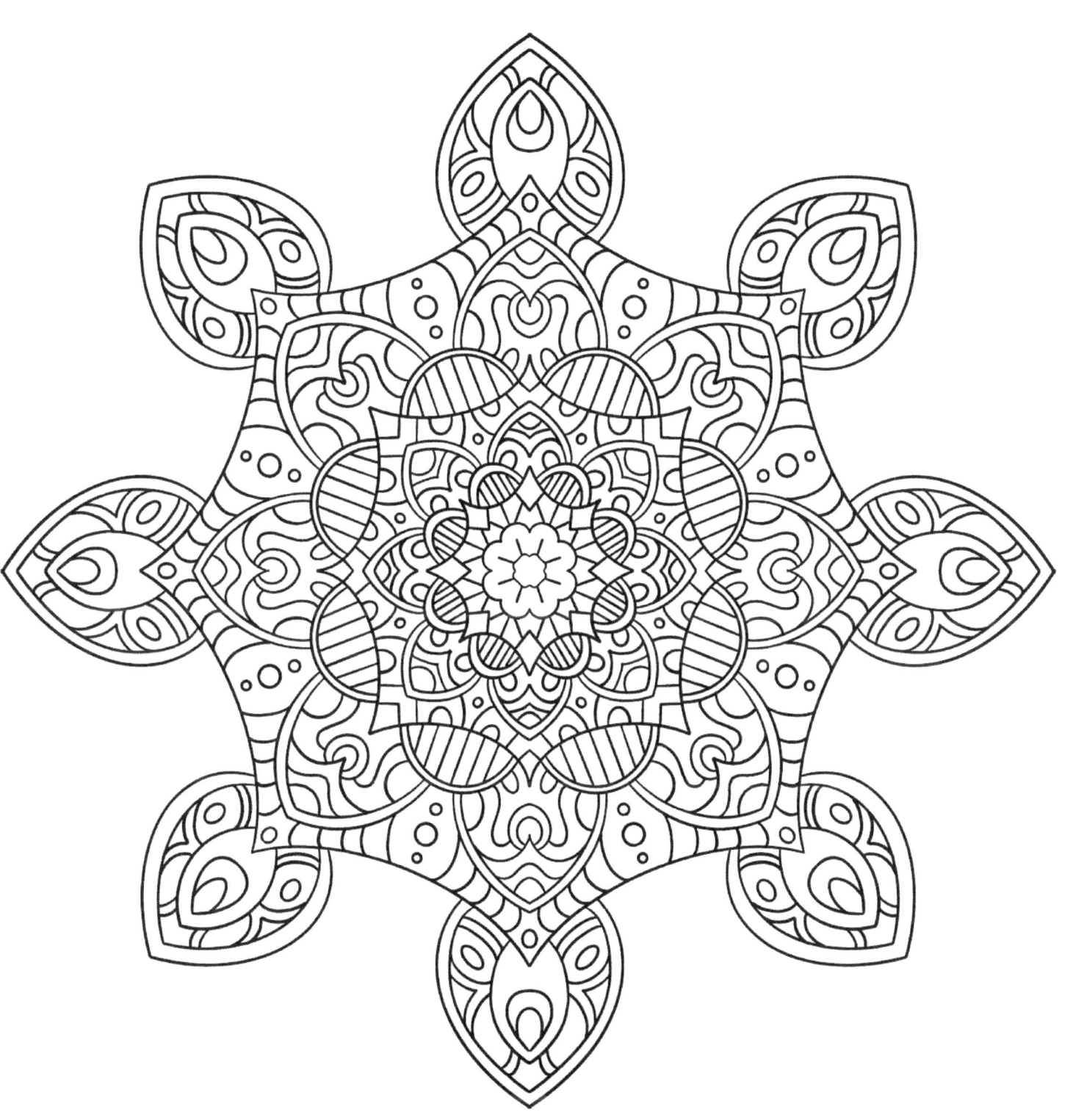

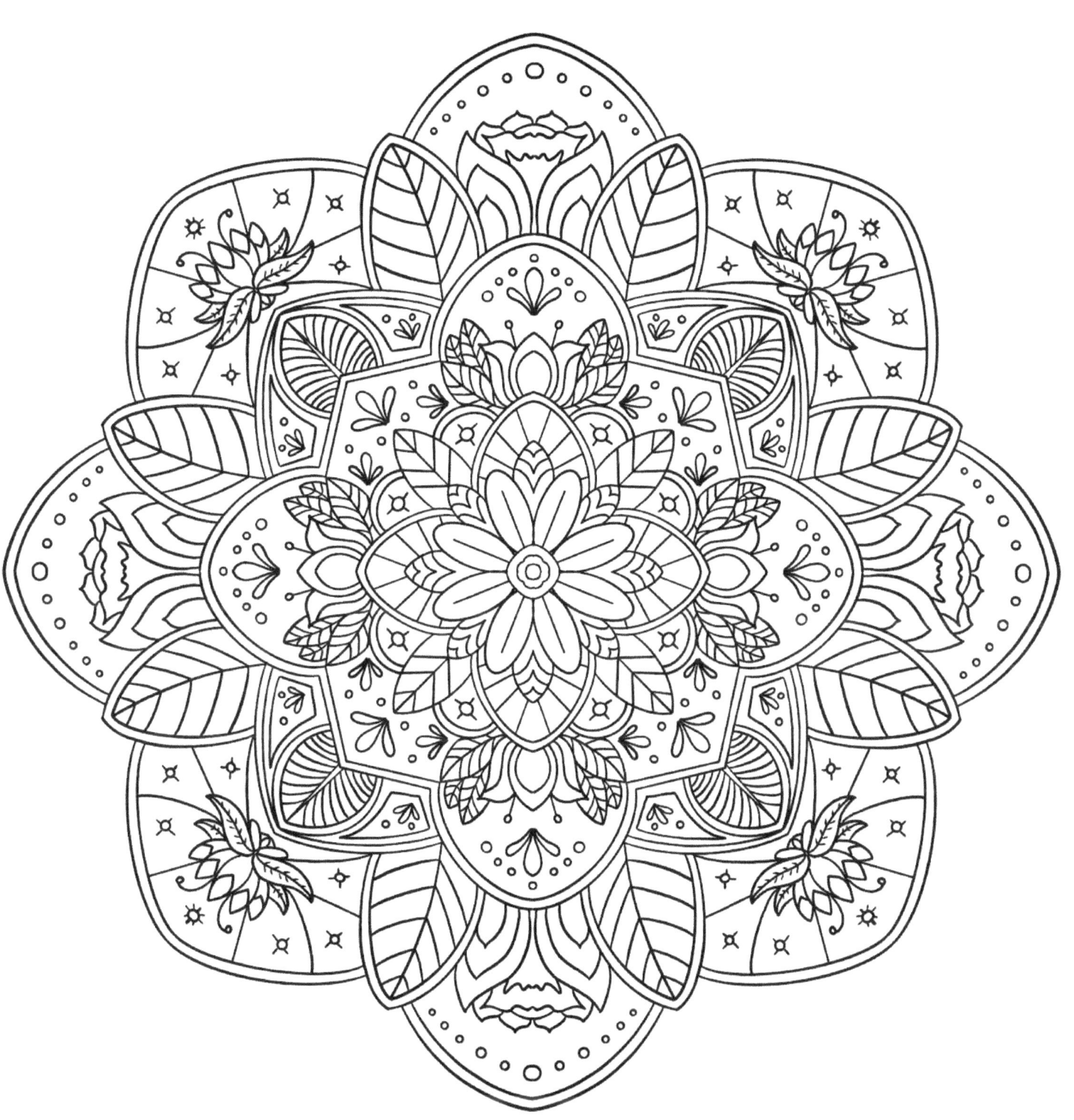

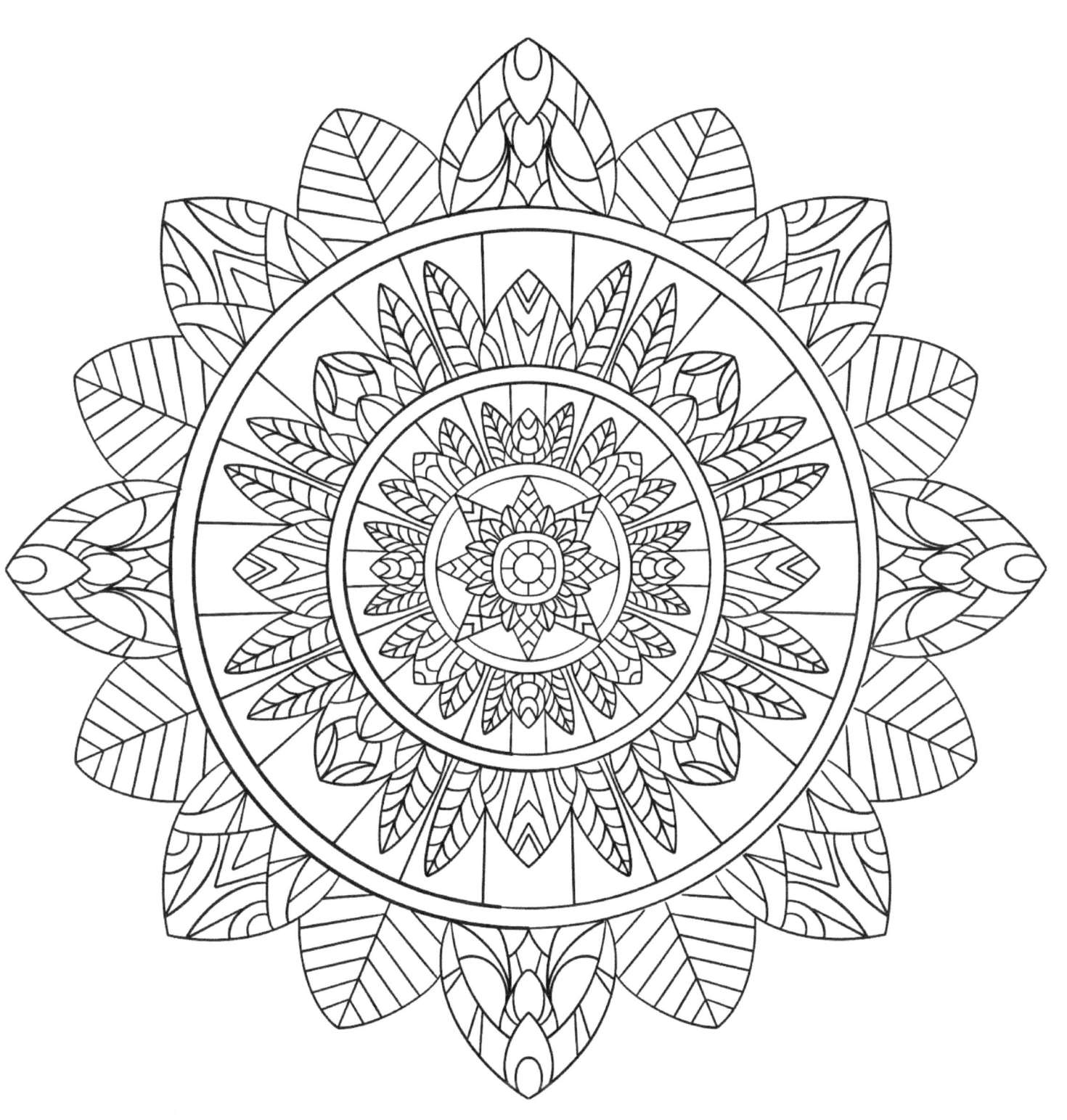

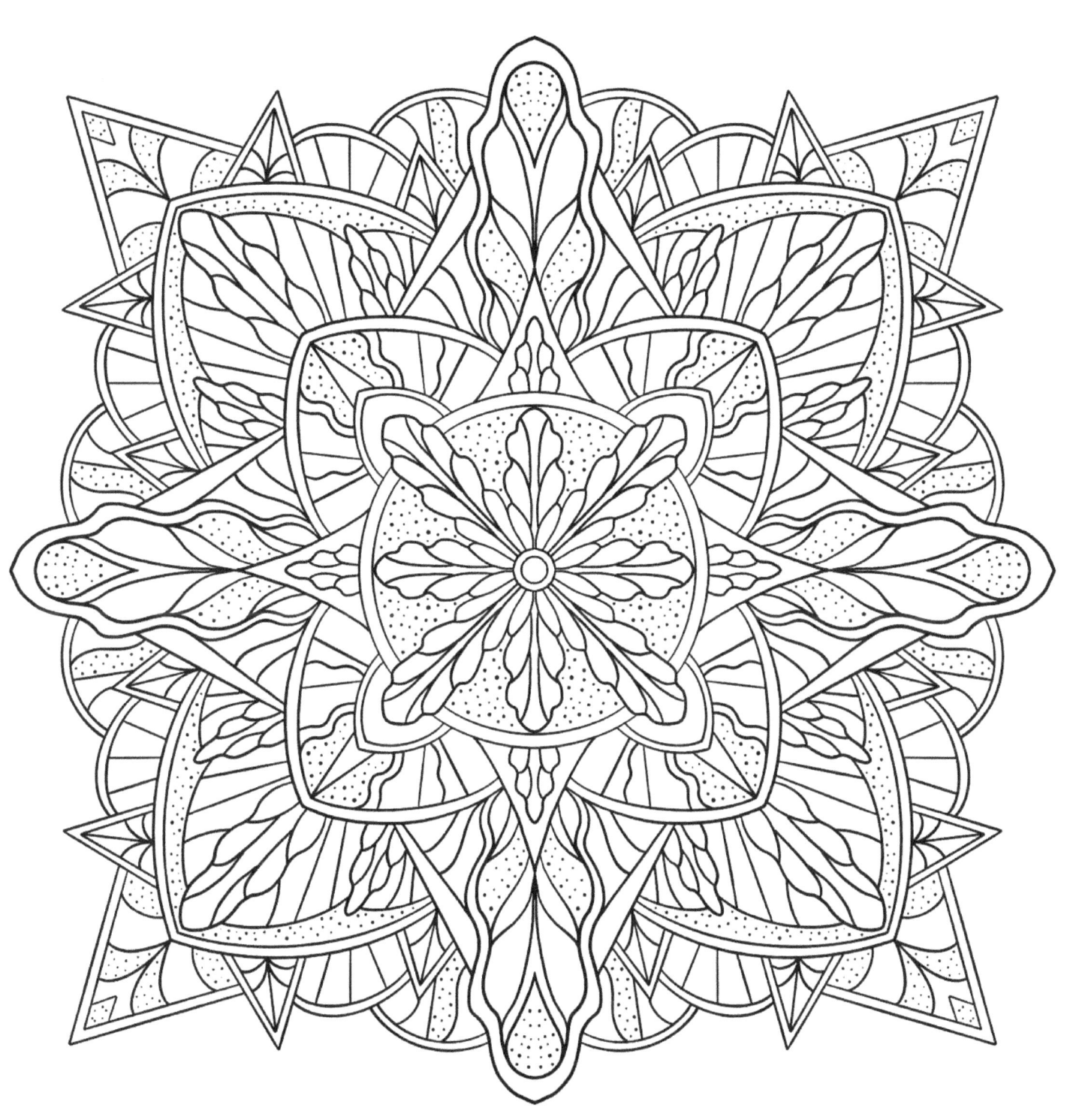

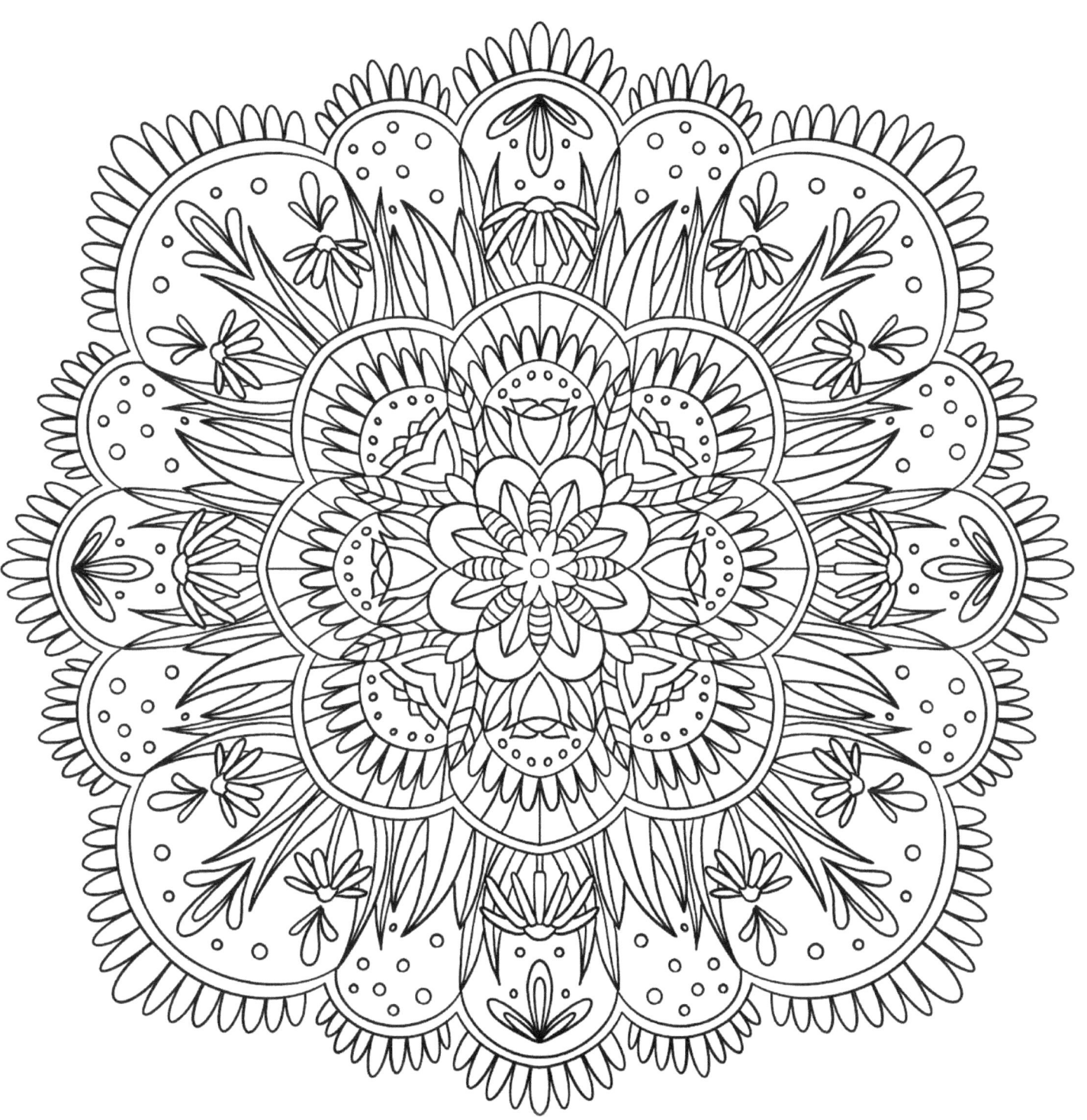

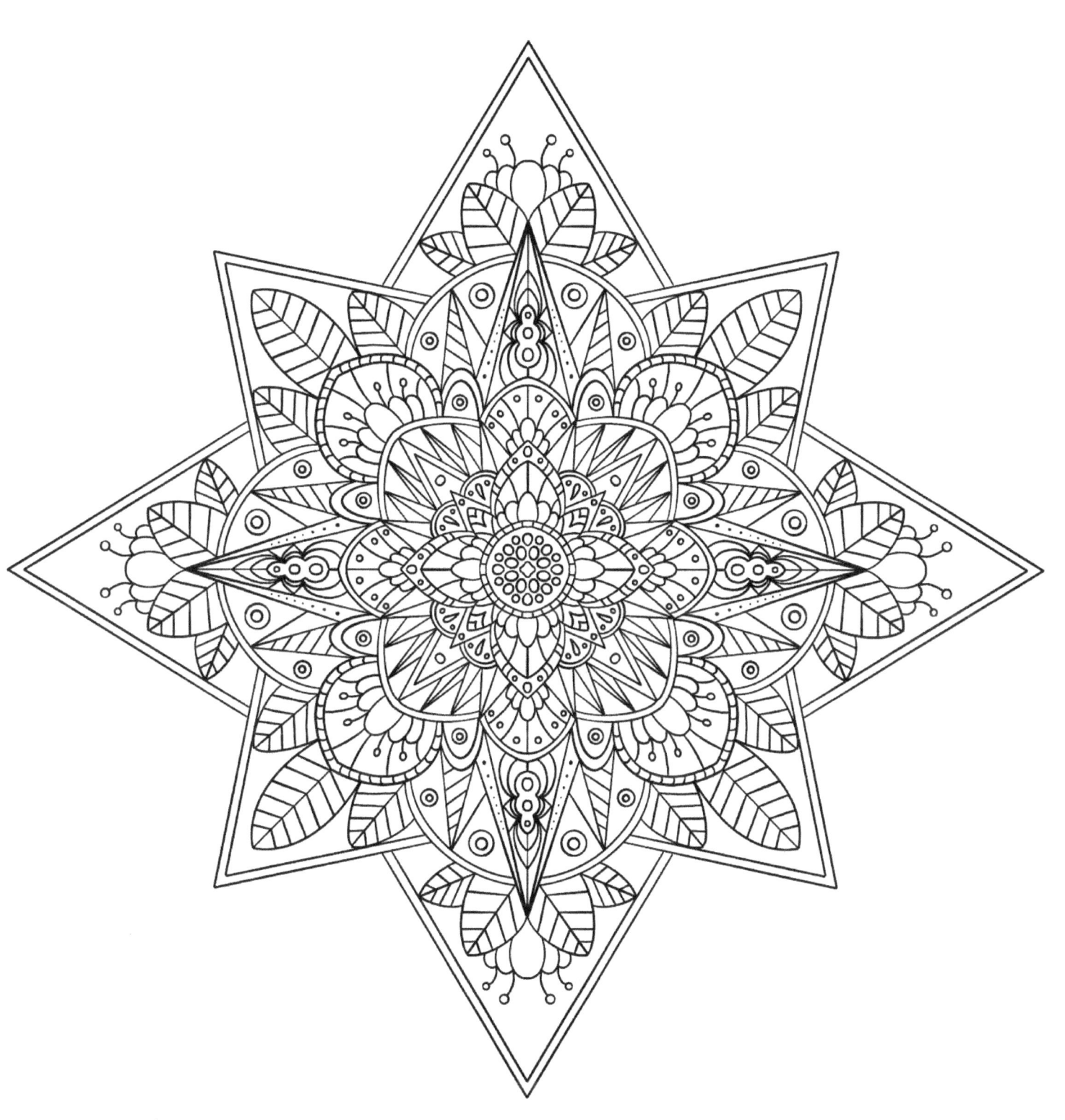

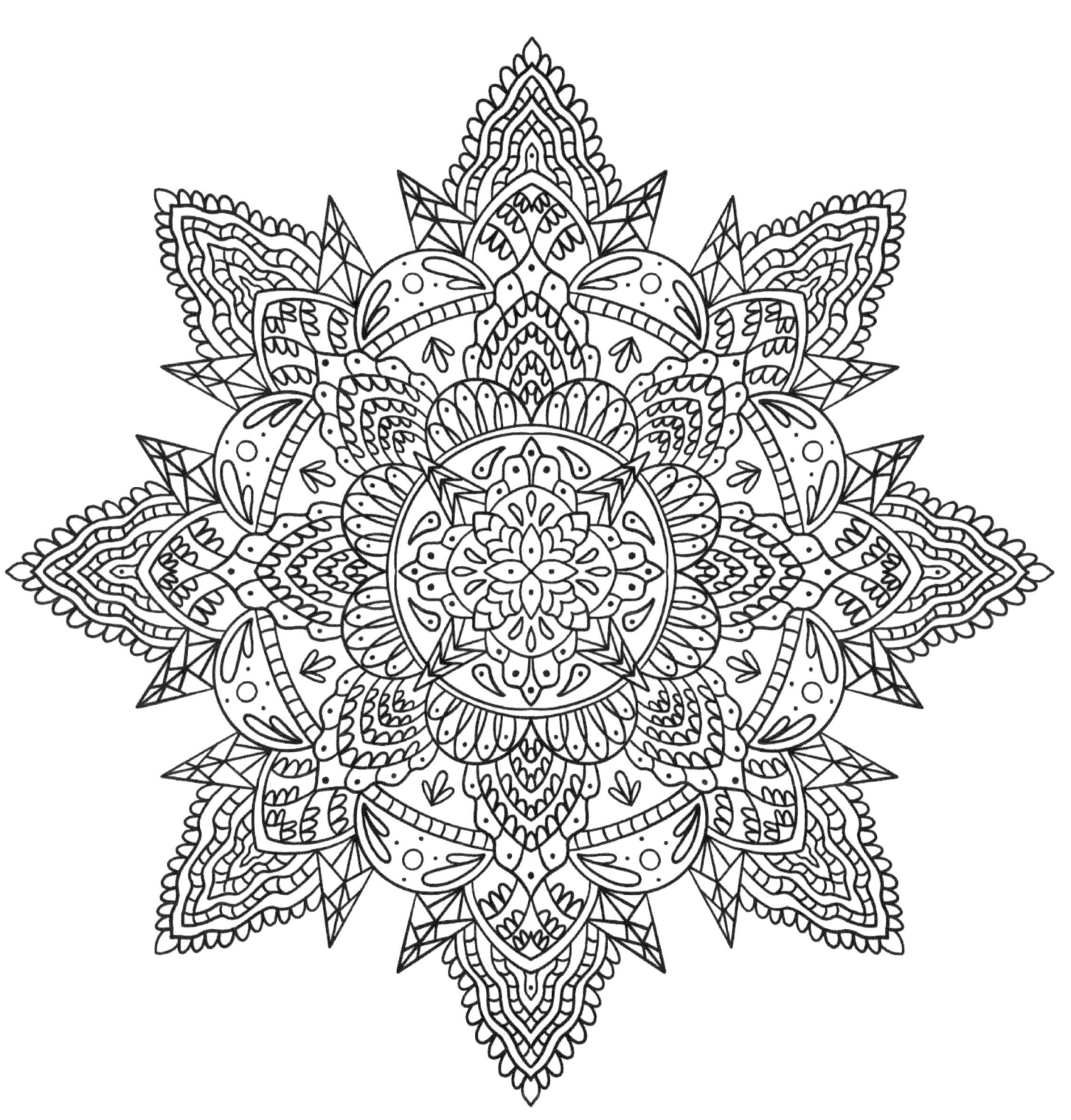

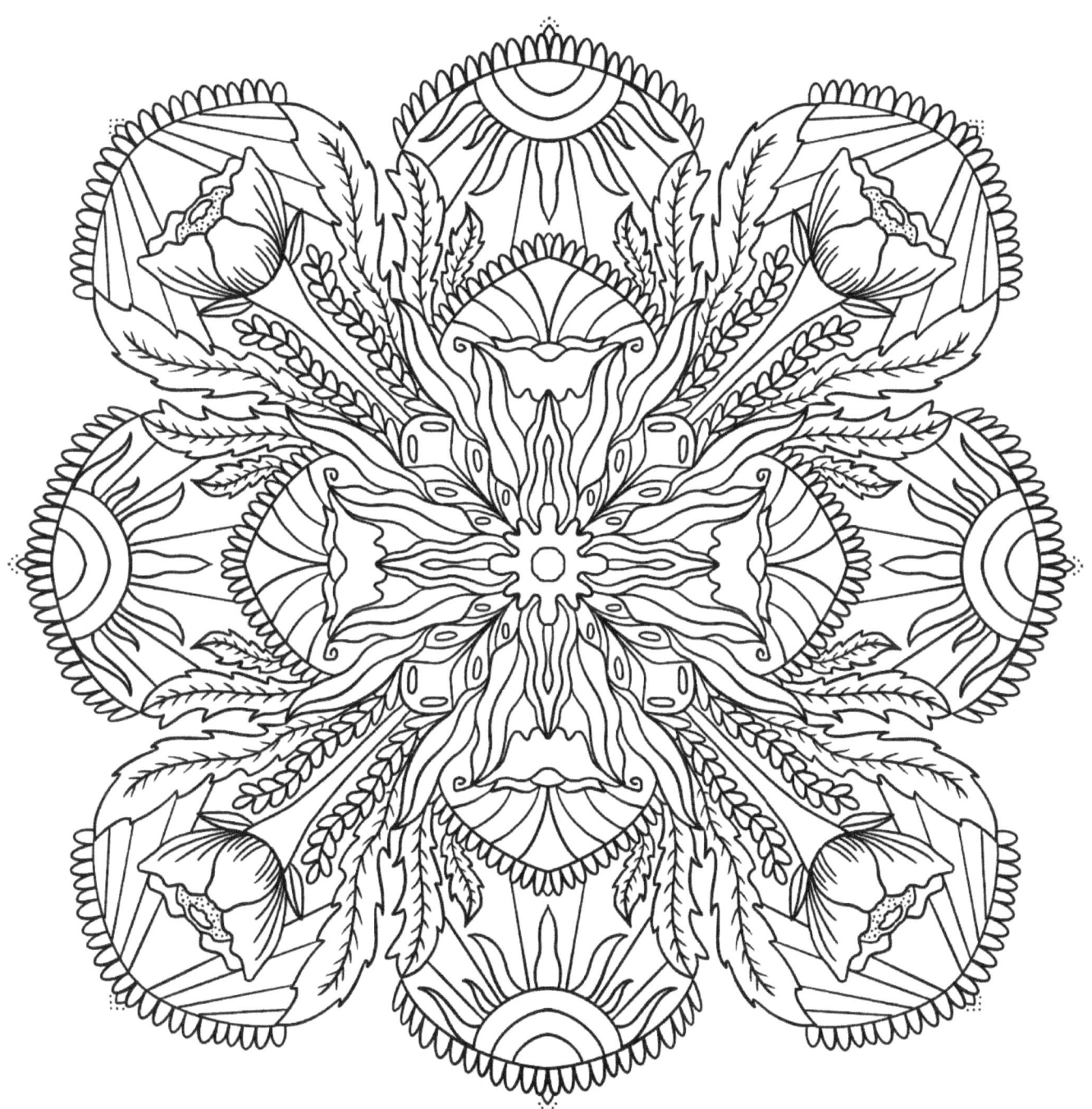

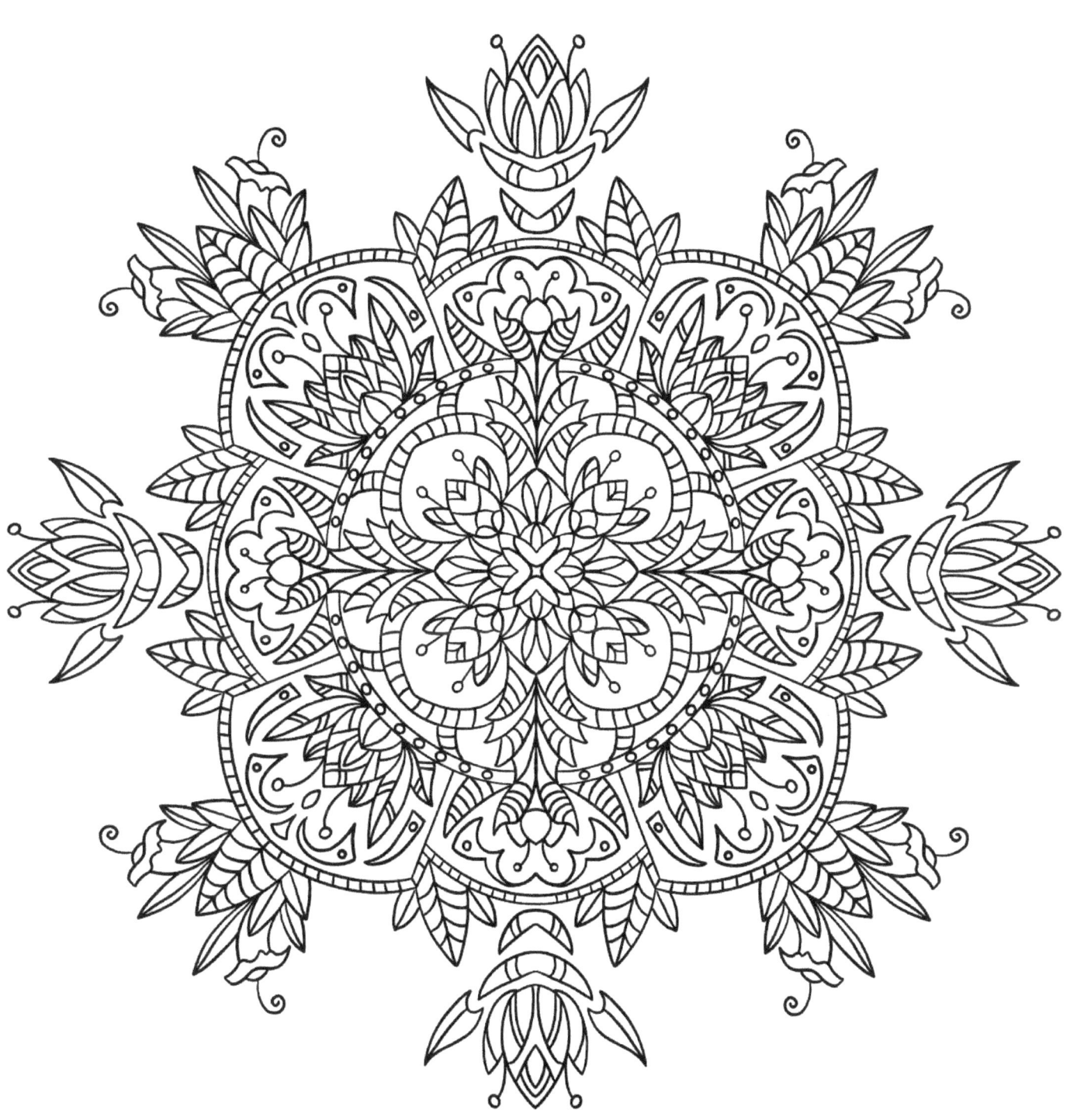

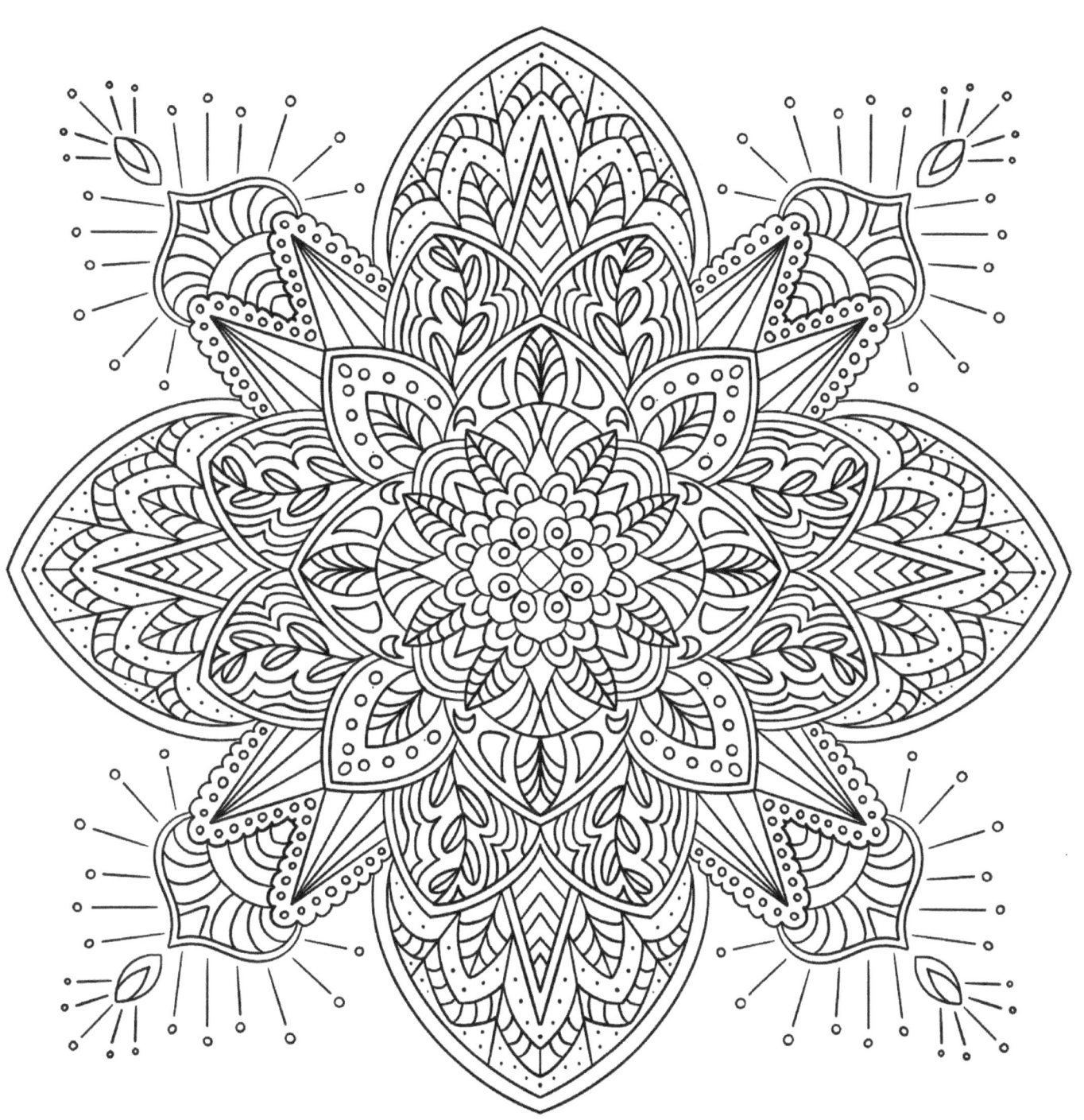

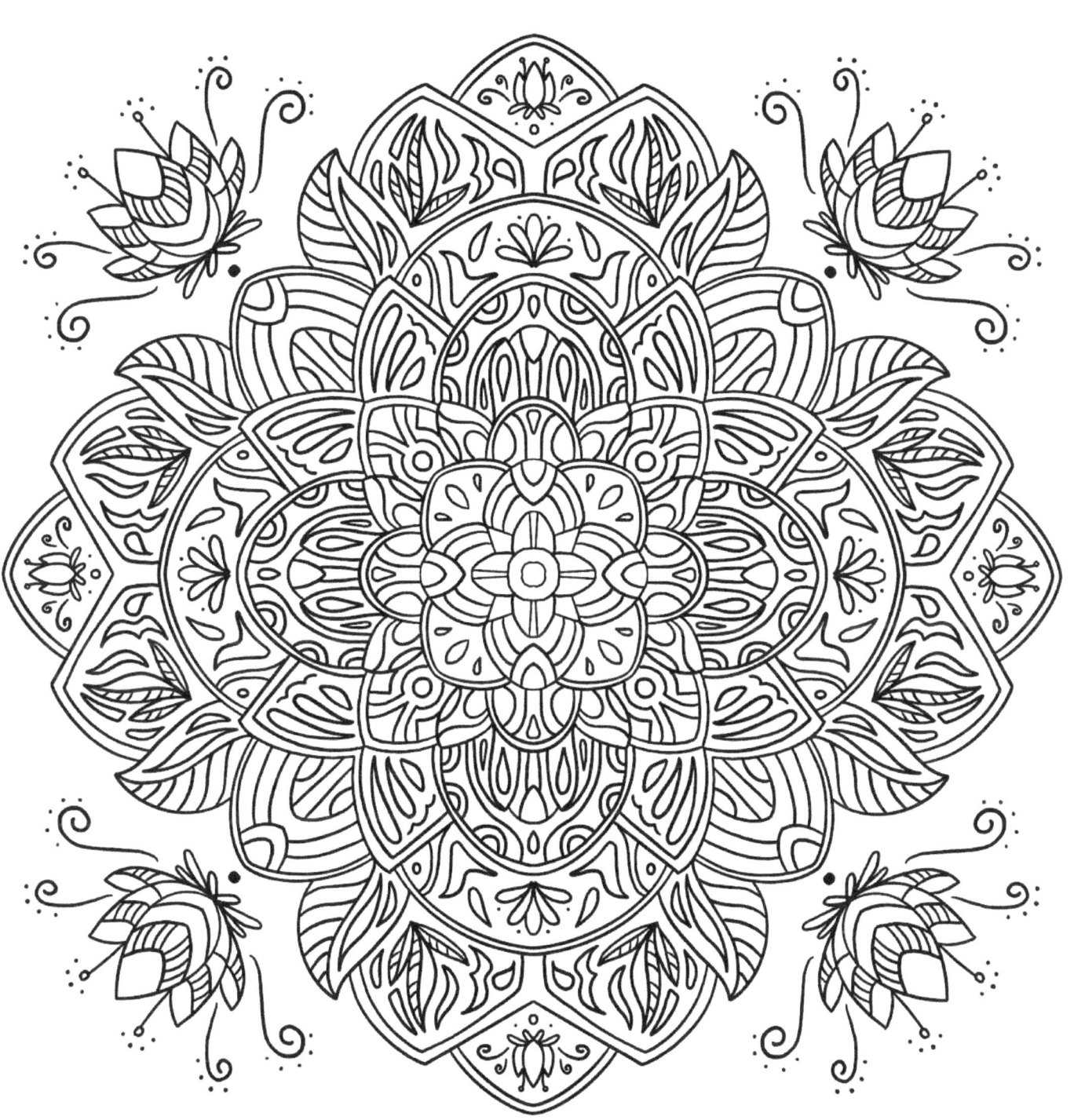

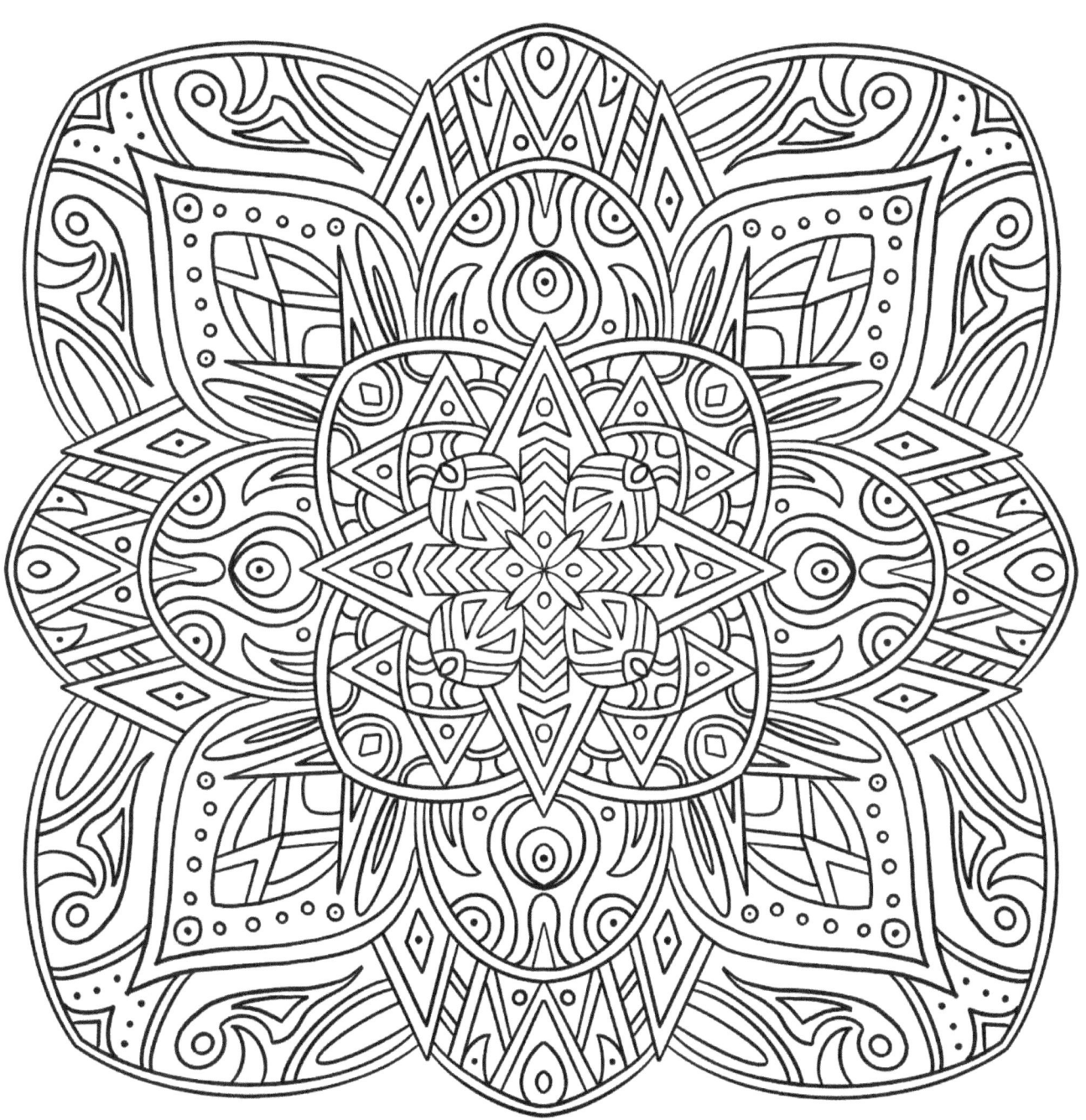

Color Tester Page

Color Tester Page